W9-AMS-440

BIG & BRIGHT BULLETIN BOARDS

Ideas That Decorate, Educate, and Motivate

Contents

The bulletin boards in this book can be made by following the detailed instructions next to each bulletin board. Each bulletin board has a suggested background color and title, a cross-referenced page number for the corresponding patterns, and a full-color illustration for easy reference. Some patterns are used in a few different bulletin boards, so be sure to make copies of the patterns, so that they may be reused. For bulletin board titles, you can use ready-made letters or cut letters from construction paper. For bulletin board borders, you can use ready-made scalloped or straight borders. To make your bulletin boards as colorful and bright as the examples provided, copy patterns on colored paper or color them with bold markers or crayons.

Credits

Authors
Amy Gamble
Lynette Pyne

Editor
Sabena Maiden

Cover Design
Julie Kinlaw

Layout Design
Jon Nawrocik

Art Coordinator
Pam Thayer

Inside Illustrations
Julie Kinlaw

Printed in the USA • All rights reserved.

ISBN 0-88724-696-6

A Slice of Good Work!

Show students just how sweet success can be! Cover the bulletin board with blue background paper. Copy the apple pattern (page 52) on yellow, green, and red construction paper. Have each student cut out and write his name on an apple pattern. Duplicate and cut out the apple slice pattern (page 50) on white paper. Color the peels of the apple slices with green, yellow, or red markers. Post examples of outstanding student work on the bulletin board. Surround the papers with rows of the personalized apples and apple slice patterns.

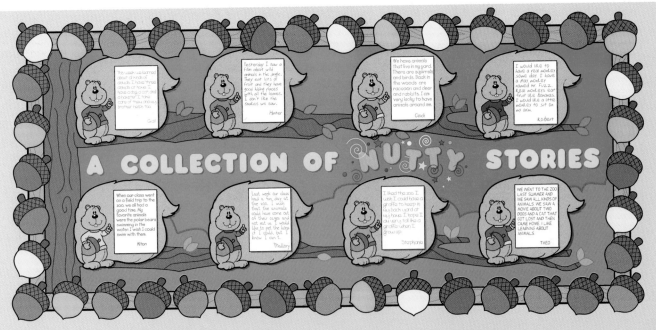

A Collection of Nutty Stories

In the fall, share the nutty side of writing! Cover the top two-thirds of the board with blue background paper for the sky and the bottom third with green background paper cut to resemble leaves. Cut out a tree with branches from brown construction paper. Display a sample of each student's work on a squirrel with large tail pattern (page 49), and use copies of the acorn pattern (page 50) to create a border.

I'm Thankful for My Students!

Show thanks for a bounty of excellent students with this harvest display. Cover the board with orange background paper. Duplicate the wheat pattern (page 51) on yellow paper. Have each student cut out and personalize a pattern with her name. Let students cut lengths of yellow paper to attach to the wheat patterns, creating wheat sheaths. Cut a large bow from fabric or wrapping paper. Attach the bow to the middle of the board, then slide the wheat stalks under it to create a sheaf.

Gobbling Good Work!

Have students strut their stuff by showing off their good work. Cover the top quarter of the board with blue background paper for the sky, and add cotton clouds. Cut strips of green paper to resemble grass and cover the bottom three-quarters of the board. Use an overhead projector to enlarge the turkey pattern (page 51) and trace on brown paper. Color, cut out, and post the large turkey on the board. Duplicate the turkey head and body pattern (page 51) on brown paper for students. Have them cut out feathers from brown, yellow, red, and orange paper and glue these to the backs of the turkey heads. Post student papers, accenting them with the turkeys.

How Would You Scare a Crow?

Let students scare each other silly with these original scarecrow designs. Cover the top third of the board with blue background paper and the bottom two-thirds with rows of green paper cut to resemble grass. Give students paper plates and have them draw unique scarecrow faces. Provide each student with a copy of the scarecrow hat pattern (page 49) to color and cut out. Assemble the scarecrows and attach each to a large wooden craft stick. Color and cut out copies of the corn (page 50) and crow (page 53) patterns, then use them to accent the display.

Our Thanksgiving Table

Give thanks with this display. Cover the top two-thirds of the board with yellow background paper and the bottom third with blue paper cut to resemble a table. Provide craft supplies and give each student a copy of the paper doll pattern (page 54) to decorate as a self-portrait. Provide copies of the pumpkin (page 53), pear (page 52), apple (page 52), corn (page 50), and pie (page 50) patterns for students to write things for which they are thankful. Display the self-portraits together around the table.

Happy Halloween!

Treat students to a festive Halloween display. Cover the top half of the board with black background paper to resemble the night sky and the bottom half with green background paper to resemble grass. Cut out a yellow paper circle to resemble the moon. Give students copies of the paper doll pattern (page 54) to decorate as Halloween self-portraits. Post the patterns on the board and label with student names. Duplicate, color, and cut out the bat pattern (page 55) and suspend each from the top of the board, attached with string and thumbtacks. Accent the sky with gold star stickers.

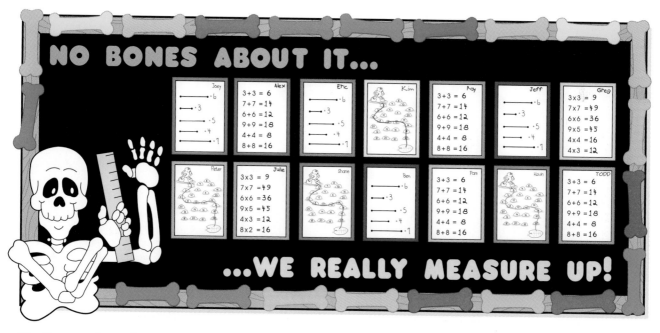

No Bones about It . . .

Encourage students to bone up on their skills, then display their work to prove it! Cover the board with black background paper. Use an overhead projector to enlarge the skeleton pattern (page 56), then cut it out. Post outstanding student work on the board along with the skeleton. Accent the work samples by placing colored construction paper behind each sample. Have students color and cut out copies of the bone pattern (page 56) to frame the display.

"Seed" What's Going On

Let others take a peek inside your classroom. Cover the top two-thirds of the board with blue background paper and the bottom third with green paper. Add white paper clouds to the top of the display. Use an overhead projector to enlarge the pumpkin pattern (page 53), then color and cut it out. Post the pumpkin and add a paper door and windows. Enlarge, color, and cut out the mouse in overalls pattern (page 52) and post it. Have students cut out pumpkin seed shapes and write class activities on them. Frame the display with the seeds.

Falling for Autumn Poetry

Let the sights of autumn inspire students' writing. Cover the top two-thirds of the board with blue background paper and the bottom third with green background paper. Add white cotton clouds. Make a brown paper tree and post it on the board. Enlarge, color, cut out, and display the happy squirrel pattern (page 55). Enlarge and cut out the leaf patterns (page 57) and have students write poems on them to post. Accent the display with extra leaf patterns.

6

Happy Kwanzaa

Celebrate the principles of Kwanzaa with this informative display. Cover the board with yellow paper. Cut out several green, red, and black triangle shapes and interlock them to create side and top borders. Add a red square to each corner. Cut seven strips of paper and write a Kwanzaa principle on each. Post these strips on the board. Make seven copies of the candle pattern (page 60) and cut out. Color three candles red, three green, and one black. Attach the candles to the bottom of the board to complete the display.

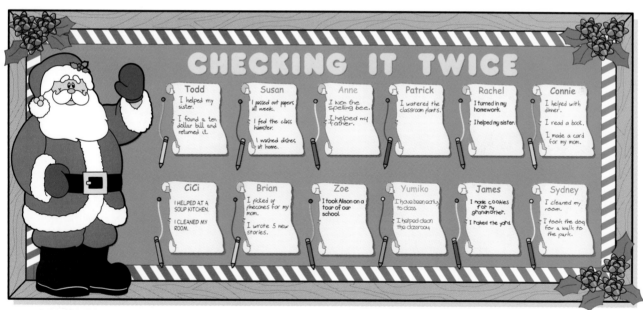

Checking It Twice

Santa Claus is on the lookout for well-behaved children. Cover the board with green paper and post a candy-cane striped border made from wrapping paper or thin red and white paper strips. Use an overhead projector to enlarge the Santa Claus pattern (page 58). Cut out the pattern and attach it to the display. Label pieces of writing paper, one with each student's name. Then, roll the top and bottom of each paper to resemble a scroll. Tack a pencil tied with string beside each paper. Have students list their good behaviors on their scrolls. Complete the display with clusters of red gift bows and green leaves to resemble holly boughs.

"Tree"rific Christmas Traditions!

Trim a bulletin board with tales of students' holiday traditions. Cover the top quarter of the board with blue background paper and the bottom three-quarters with white background paper cut to resemble snowdrifts. Give each child a copy of the evergreen tree pattern (page 62). Have students color and cut out the patterns, then write on them about Christmas traditions. Post the trees and top them with large foil stars. Tear and attach pieces of white and blue tissue paper to create falling snow. Make a border by attaching student-made snowflakes to the edges of the display.

Happy Hanukkah

Share stories of Hanukkah memories. Cover the board with blue background paper. Cut long strips of yellow paper to create a Star of David and post it on the board. Students can make dreidels using the sides of dreidel patterns (page 60). Add a spinner to each dreidel by gluing a craft stick to the top and a paper triangle to the bottom. Add the dreidels to the posted Hanukkah memories. Complete the display by attaching yellow paper stars to the edges of the board and blue and white stars to the background.

Sugar and Spice . . .

Success never tasted so sweet! Cover the top third of the board with blue background paper. On white background paper, add a thin layer of glue and sprinkle glitter to resemble snow. Use the glitter paper to cover the bottom two-thirds of the board. Make copies of the gingerbread house pattern (page 61) for each student to cut out and decorate with crayons, candy, glitter, and buttons. Label the patterns with students' names, then use them to accent student papers. Create a border with decorated candy cane patterns (page 59).

Happy New Year!

Ring in the New Year with this timely display. Cover the board with yellow background paper. Use an overhead projector to enlarge the Baby New Year pattern (page 63). Color and cut out the pattern, then post it on the board. Give each student a copy of the clock pattern (page 63) on which to write a resolution or New Year's promise. Display the clocks on the board. Accent the display by attaching construction paper confetti and stars. Create an interesting border by twisting strips of crepe paper and attaching them to the edges of the display.

The Snowman Has . . .

Create a winter wonderland of cool friends. Cover the board with dark blue background paper. Give each student a paper plate and copies of the top hat and bow tie patterns (page 59) to create unique snowmen using cotton balls, pom-poms, buttons, sequins, and glitter. Attach the top hat and bow tie to the snowmen's faces with glue or staples, then display the snowmen on the board. Provide copies of the snowflake pattern (page 64) for students to use to write descriptions of their frosty friends. Create a snowfall by gluing cotton balls to the board.

Dive into Adventure

Slip and slide your way through winter writing adventures. Cover the board with white background paper. Cut out blue plastic wrap and post to resemble ocean waves among ice caps. Give each student a copy of the penguin pattern (page 65) to color and cut out. Have students write winter adventure stories on the patterns, then post them on the board. Accent the display by having students draw fish on the ice caps. Create a shiny border for the display using strips of aluminum foil.

Bundle Up for Winter Fun!

Chill out with this winter weather scene. Cover the top quarter of the board with blue background paper and the bottom three-quarters with white background paper cut to resemble snowdrifts. Cut a piece of aluminum foil and attach it to the board to make a frozen pond. Provide each student with a copy of the paper doll pattern (page 54) and winter coat, boots, and winter hat patterns (page 67) to color, cut out, and post on the board. Draw skis, sleds, snowmen, and ice skates to accent the winter scene. Complete the display by adding paper trees and icicle top and bottom borders cut from aluminum foil.

Lovely Work!

Students will love seeing their work on display. Cover the board with pink background paper. Use an overhead projector to enlarge the valentine bear pattern (page 66). Color and cut out the pattern and post it on the board. Copy the candy heart pattern (page 64) and give one to each student to color, cut out, and label with his name. Cut out and decorate several large paper hearts and post them on the board to highlight student papers, then accent the papers with the personalized candy hearts. Complete the display by creating a lace border using half-circle shapes cut from white paper.

Everything's Coming Up Roses!

Growing good skills has never been easier! Cover the top half of the board with blue background paper and the bottom half with green paper strips cut to resemble grass. Add white paper clouds and an enlarged copy of the turtle with watering can pattern (page 69) to the display. Design a trellis from strips of white paper and attach it to the center of the board. Post examples of student work on the trellis. Accent the display with roses made from tissue paper, chenille craft sticks, and copies of the elm leaf pattern (page 57).

High Flying Fun

Let students' imaginations soar. Cover the bulletin board with blue background paper and attach clouds cut from white paper. Make two copies of the bird pattern (page 68), then color and cut out each. Cut a banner from colored paper and attach it to the board with the display title inside, then accent it with the bird patterns. Make kites by cutting out paper diamonds for students to post spring adventure stories. Provide yarn, ribbons, and other craft materials for students to decorate the kites.

Hoppy Spring!

Leap into spring with this pond display. Cover the board with blue background paper. Add a large lily pad cut from green paper and smaller lily pads by cutting triangle notches into green paper plates. Write upcoming class events on the plates. Cut out and color copies of the sitting frog pattern (page 68) and leaping frog pattern (page 73) to attach to the board. Make cattails with rolled sheets of brown paper attached to green strips of paper at the bottom and a pipe cleaner at the top. Water lilies can be cut from paper and glued to green paper plates.

A Shower of Good News

Brighten up rainy spring days with this cheerful bulletin board. Cover the board with blue background paper. Design a rainbow from strips of colored paper or draw one using markers or paint. Accent the scene with a decorated sun pattern (page 102) and copies of the cloud pattern (page 71). Give each student a copy of the umbrella pattern (page 71) to color and cut out. On the umbrella patterns, have students write about special class events. Display them on the board. Create a rain shower effect by cutting out and coloring several copies of the raindrop pattern (page 71) and displaying lengths of blue yarn on the board.

Growing Good Habits

Cultivate good behavior with this bulletin board. Cover the top section of the board with a strip of blue background paper. Make a picket fence section by posting white paper strips cut with pointed tops. Attach a grass background section by cutting notches in sheets of green paper. Layer sheets of brown paper cut to resemble a garden. Enlarge, color, cut out, and post the gardening rabbit pattern (page 75). Color and cut out several copies of the carrot pattern (page 73). Post each with a classroom rule. Accent the display using tissue paper flowers with chenille craft stick stems.

Spring Is Hatching

Make an "egg"cellent display. Cover the top third of the board with blue background paper and the bottom two-thirds with green paper. Enlarge the barn pattern (page 72) with an overhead projector. Then, color, cut out, and post it. Add purple paper strips to create a fence. Copy the egg pattern (page 75) on yellow and white paper for students to cut out. Students can draw faces on the yellow eggs and trace their handprints on colorful paper for wings. Then, cut the white eggs into broken eggshells. Post the hatched chicks.

Treat Yourself to a Happy Easter!

Hop to it and get your class thinking about Easter. Cover the board with purple background paper. Add a strip of green paper to the bottom cut to resemble grass. Enlarge the bunny with egg pattern (page 74), then color, cut out, and attach it to the middle of the board. Give each student a copy of the Easter basket pattern (page 74) and the egg pattern (page 75) to color and cut out. On the egg patterns, have students write their favorite Easter activities. Attach the eggs and baskets to the board. Decorate additional copies of the egg pattern for a festive border.

Help Find the Lucky Clover!

Students will find fun in this bulletin board. Cover the top half of the board with blue background paper for a sky and the bottom with green background paper cut to resemble sloping hills. Post small cotton-ball clouds and a large, light blue paper cloud. Create a rainbow by attaching twisted strips of crepe paper from the large cloud to the edge of the board. Use an overhead projector to enlarge the leprechaun pattern (page 70) and post. Color and cut out several copies of the shamrock pattern (page 69) and one four-leaf clover pattern (page 68). Attach the shamrock patterns to the board, hiding the four-leaf clover for the class to find.

Butterflies Color Our World

Set students' imaginations flying by letting them help create this unique display. Cover the board with blue background paper. Cut several bushes from green paper and place them along the bottom of the display. Give each student a copy of the butterfly pattern (page 79) to decorate and cut out. Attach the butterflies to the scene. Make "butterfly trails" using colored chalk or lengths of yarn. Enhance the display with a bottom edge border made from paper or silk flowers.

I Spot Good Work!

Great papers won't be hard to spot on this student work display. Cover the board with red background paper. Cut several large circles (approximately 12-inch diameter) and a few small circles from black paper or felt. Attach the circles to the board to create spots. Inside each large spot, display a student paper. Then, give each student a copy of the bug pattern (page 76) to color and cut out. Accent the display by making a bug border.

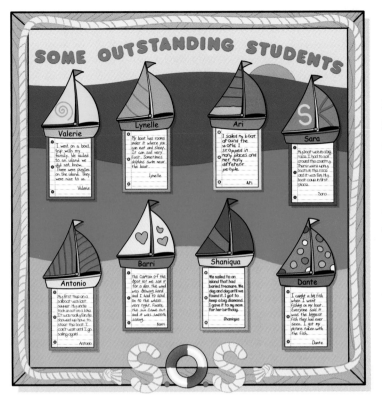

Some Outstanding Students

Set sail and show off some exceptional work. Cover the board with sections of light, medium, and dark blue background paper. Cut out an orange circle and tuck it behind one section to create a sunset. Provide students with copies of the sailboat pattern (page 80) to decorate, cut out, and personalize. Frame student papers with colored construction paper and post on the board. Accent the student papers with the decorated sailboats. Create a border for the display using lengths of rope, raffia, or yellow paper. Add the title "S.O.S.," coloring the letter "O" to resemble a life preserver.

Swim into Summer

Dive into summer fun with this underwater adventure bulletin board. Cover the board with blue background paper. Create waves by attaching blue scalloped paper border across the top of the display. Attach orange and tan scalloped paper border along the bottom of the board to create an ocean floor. Use lengths of green, twisted crepe paper to make strands of seaweed. Enlarge the diver pattern (page 83) and attach it to the board. Give each child a copy of the fish pattern (page 79) to color, cut out, and label with her name. Accent the scene by making coral and sea anemone from tissue paper and cutting starfish from construction paper.

Friends Are Cool!

Friends are forever, as this bulletin board shows. Cover the board with blue background paper. Give each student a copy of the ice pop pattern (page 77) to color and cut out. Let each student draw and label a picture of himself and a friend on the ice pop. Post the patterns on the board. Add large wooden craft sticks to the bottoms of the patterns. Create a cool border by cutting ice cube shapes from white and blue paper. Highlight the display with accents of glitter glue on the ice cubes and the bulletin board background.

On the Trail of Good Work!

March along with great work! Cover the board with green paper. Attach a strip of tan paper cut to create a curved path across the center. Copy, color, and cut out the ant 1, ant 2, and ant 3 patterns (page 76-78) and post them along the path. Frame student papers with construction paper and place above each ant. Enlarge the picnic basket pattern (page 78). Then, color, cut out, personalize, and post it. Accent the display with paper flowers. Finish with a white, pink, and red square paper border.

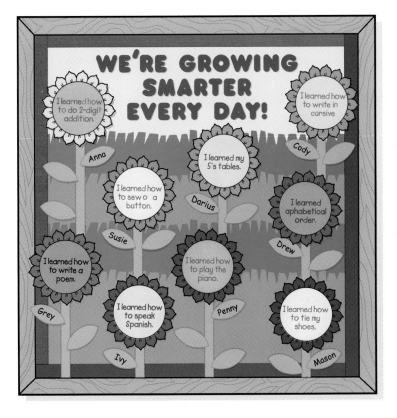

We're Growing Smarter Every Day!

Praise students' blossoming skills with this display. Cover the top quarter of the board with blue background paper and the bottom three-quarters with green paper strips cut to resemble grass. Give each student a copy of the flower pattern (page 85) to color and cut out. Inside the flowers, have students write new skills they have learned. Attach the flowers to the display, adding stems and leaves cut from paper. Personalize the flowers by writing students' names on the leaves.

Packing for Paradise

Get the class dreaming about summer. Cover the top half of the board with blue background paper and the bottom half with brown background paper cut to resemble a sandy beach. Create waves by attaching dark and light blue scalloped paper in layers. Copy, color, and cut out the sun pattern (page 102) and the cloud pattern (page 71) and post. Enlarge, color, and cut out the palm tree pattern (page 80) and attach it to the display. Enlarge copies of the suitcase pattern (page 105) for students to color and cut out. Then, have students write about what they would bring with them to an island. Display the student writing.

Reflecting on Summer

Reminisce about fun summer days with this cool display. Cover the board with thick strips of light and dark yellow background paper. Cut a large sun from yellow and orange paper, then color, cut out, and attach a copy of the sunglasses pattern (page 84) to the sun. Post the sun on the display. Give each student a copy of the sunglasses pattern to decorate and cut out. Under each pair of sunglasses, post a student story about a favorite summer memory. Accent the display by cutting letters from aluminum foil for portions of the title.

Pearls of Wisdom

Let students share words of wisdom with next year's class. Cover the top half of the board with blue paper and the bottom half with brown paper cut to look like an ocean floor. Use an overhead projector to enlarge the treasure chest pattern (page 82), and color and attach it to the board. Give students copies of the oyster shell pattern (page 82) to color, cut out, and write words of advice for the upcoming class. Then, glue a table-tennis ball to the center of each oyster. Add a pearl border made from white foam balls.

Congratulations Graduates

Recognize students' achievements with this distinguished display. Cover the board with aluminum foil and create a layered border using scalloped and straight paper strips. Enlarge the graduation ribbon pattern (page 81) using an overhead projector. Color the ribbon and post it on the board. Make nameplates from colored paper and label them with student names. Cut large plaque screws from yellow paper and add details with black marker. Then, post them in the corners of the display.

Hang on!

Swing into summer with this whimsical countdown display. Cover the board with blue background paper. Create vines by attaching twisted strips of brown paper and attaching them to the top of the board. Enlarge copies of the monkey pattern (page 81), then color and cut out. Attach a specified number of monkeys (for example, a monkey to represent each of the last ten days of school) to the vine and number the monkeys with index cards. Each day remove a monkey from the board and adjust the number in the title. Accent the display by adding a border of leaves cut from green paper.

Become a Stellar Speller!

Reward spelling superstars with this sparkling display. Cover the board with dark blue background paper. Enlarge and make copies of the star pattern (page 85) and write a spelling word activity on each. Copy the star pattern and label one for each student. When a student demonstrates mastery or shows great improvement with spelling, post his star on the board or place all of the stars on the board and attach star stickers to reward good grades. Accent the display with enlarged copies of the star with face pattern (page 85).

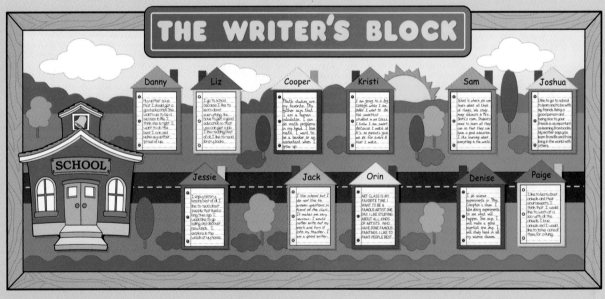

The Writer's Block

Show students that their work is "write on." Cover the top quarter of the board with light blue paper and the bottom three-fourths with green paper. Draw trees, bushes, and a sun to create the landscape. Add cotton-ball clouds and a road using black paper strips and a yellow paint pen. Enlarge the schoolhouse pattern (page 86), then color and cut it out. Create a personalized house for each student's work by posting sheets of paper with triangles for roofs and rectangles for chimneys.

START ON THE "WRITE" FOOT.

1. Choose a topic.
2. Organize your ideas.
3. Write a first draft.
4. Share your paper with someone else.
5. Edit.
6. Write a final draft.
7. Publish and illustrate.

Start on the "Write" Foot

Help students get in step with writing. Cover the board with green background paper. Create a border using strips of brown paper with white chalk lines drawn to resemble a track. Enlarge, color, cut out, and post copies of the hippo pattern (page 88) at the bottom of the board. Copy, color, and cut out the pencil pattern (page 84) and number each. On sentence strips, write the steps of the writing process and post them beside each pencil. Accent the display with pennants made from colored paper.

Spotlight on Good Books

Give good books a special spotlight. Cover the top half of the board with black background paper and the bottom half with blue background paper. Cut two large circles and two large triangles from yellow paper. Create spotlights by attaching the triangles to the board, then overlapping the circles at the bottom. Attach pieces of fabric to each side of the board, then tie them back with lengths of fabric to form curtain swags. Cut a curtain valance from matching fabric for the top of the display. Enlarge, color, and cut out the tuxedo bear pattern (page 88) and attach it to the middle of the board. Inside the spotlights, post student book reports and reviews.

Nouns, Verbs, Adjectives and Adverbs

Put a twist on learning the parts of speech. Cover the top two-thirds of the board with light blue background paper and the bottom third with green paper cut to resemble grass. Add white paper clouds. Use an overhead projector to enlarge the baseball cap pattern (page 86) and rhino pattern (page 87). Then, color, cut out, and post them. Use different colors for each part of speech word in the title. Cut out paper speech balloons and write descriptions of the scene, color-coding each part of speech to match the title.

Be a Top-Notch Editor

Nothing will get past your eagle-eyed editors when they follow this checklist. Cover the board with green background paper to resemble a chalkboard. Enlarge the apple pattern (page 52) and teacher mouse pattern (page 87), then color and cut out each one. Post the patterns on the display. Using colored chalk, write a checklist for student editors. Next to the checklist, post proofreader's marks written on a large sheet of chart paper. Accent the display with a chalkboard eraser cut from paper.

Punctuation Pointers

Point out the importance of proper punctuation with this helpful bulletin board. Cover the board with yellow background paper. Use an overhead projector to enlarge the pencil pattern (page 84). On each eraser section, draw a punctuation mark. On each pencil, write a description telling when and how the punctuation mark is used. Create a handy student reference by posting the patterns on the board.

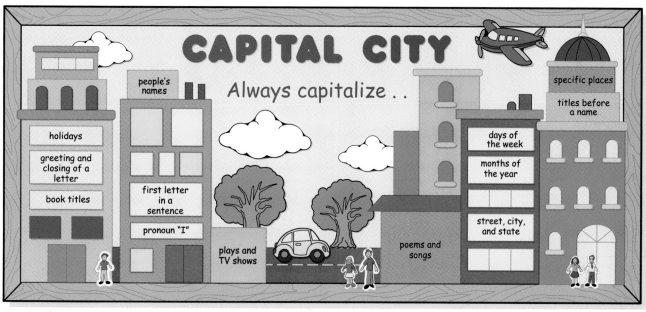

Capital City

Encourage students to capitalize correctly with this reference designed to improve their skills. Cover the board with light blue background paper, adding a strip of gray paper and small yellow strips to the bottom to make a city street. Create city buildings by cutting squares and rectangles from colored paper, then overlapping and attaching them to the board. Write capitalization rules inside the building windows. Accent the display by coloring and cutting out copies of the cloud pattern (page 71), simple tree pattern (page 100), car pattern (page 103), and airplane pattern (page 105). Use markers to draw details on the buildings.

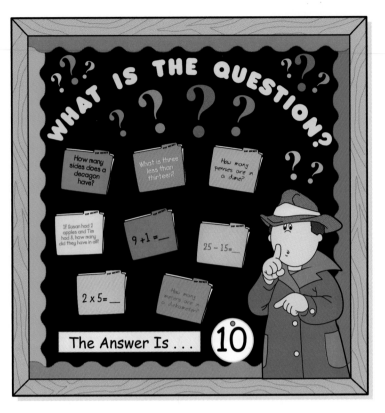

What Is the Question?

Put agents on the lookout for secret math information. Cover the board with black background paper. Use an overhead projector to enlarge the secret agent and file folder patterns (page 89), then color and attach them to the display. At the bottom of the board, post a word, phrase, or number "answer." Let students write possible questions related to the answer on the folder patterns. Post the folders on the board. Change the answers each week and challenge students to write new questions to match.

Nail Down Your Facts

After hammering away with math facts practice, reward students by displaying their efforts on this bulletin board. Cover the board with yellow background paper. Create wood texture by drawing a wood grain pattern on several strips of red and brown paper, then use them to make a display border and student nameplates. Enlarge, color, and cut out the construction mouse pattern (page 91) and attach it to the board. Under each nameplate, post a sheet of paper indicating who has learned what math facts.

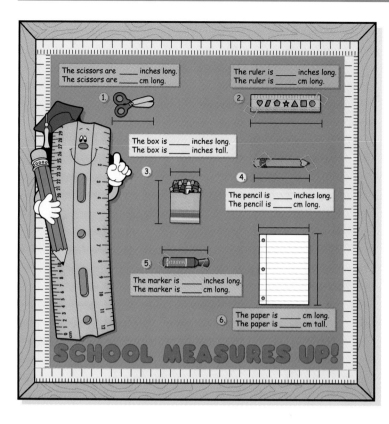

School Measures Up!

Students will go to great lengths to complete this challenge. Cover the board with green background paper. Create a ruler border by drawing tick lines on several strips of yellow paper, and attaching them to the edges of the board. Enlarge the ruler with face pattern (page 90) using an overhead projector. Color and cut out the pattern, then post. Attach an assortment of classroom objects, such as pencils, paper, scissors, and crayons, to the board for students to measure. Post laminated strips of paper under each object for students to record their measurements.

Check Out Our Numbers!

Any way you count it, this display will be a hit! Cover the board with blue background paper. Use an overhead projector to enlarge the boy with sign pattern (page 90). Then, color, cut out, and attach the pattern to the display. Have each student draw a self-portrait on a sheet of paper. Around the pictures, have students write numbers reflecting their age, height, address, room number, etc. Display the papers on the board in frames made from colored paper. Use lengths of string and thumbtacks to complete the framed pictures. Make several copies of the smiley face pattern (page 91), then color and label each with a number to make a border.

Which Do You Like More?

The votes are in! Cover the board with yellow background paper. Create a border for the display using colored paper or fabric squares. Attach three large paper rectangles to the display. Copy, color, and cut out the hamburger, (page 93) pizza slice (page 93), and ice cream cone patterns (page 92) and post them in the rectangles. Use photos of each student or have students draw self-portraits, then label them with their names. Allow students to vote by tacking their photos next to their selections. Change the display by placing new objects to vote on in the rectangles.

Cuckoo for Clocks!

Tick-tock … it's time to learn about telling time. Cover the board with green background paper. Use an overhead projector to enlarge the cuckoo clock pattern (page 94). Color, cut out, and post it. Enlarge copies of the clock hands (page 91) and clock face (page 93) patterns and assemble them using paper fasteners. Provide index cards and toothpicks for students to glue together to make digital time cards. Set the clock hands to various times, so students can match them. Attach an envelope with additional time cards.

Get in Shape!

Keep students' math skills in top shape with this idea. Cover the board with blue background paper. Cut a large triangle, circle, rectangle, and square from colored paper. Post the shapes on the board and label each. Copy, color, and cut out the sailboat (page 80), pizza slice (page 93), and clock face (page 93) patterns. Place the patterns on the appropriate shapes. Have students add to the display by attaching magazine pictures, drawings, or real objects inside the appropriate shapes. Complete the bulletin board by making a border from smaller paper shapes.

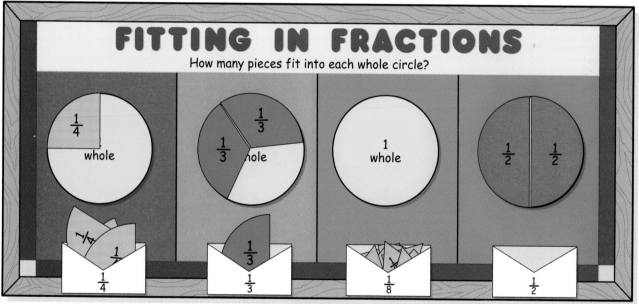

Fitting in Fractions

Help students piece together fractions. Cover the top of the board with yellow background paper. Cover the rest of the board with four sheets of colored paper. Make four enlarged copies of the divided circle pattern (page 92) and label each "1 whole." Attach one circle to each piece of colored paper and add several hook-and-loop squares to each one. Make several more identically-sized copies of the divided circle pattern and cut them out using the fractions guides. Laminate the fraction pieces and attach hook-and-loop squares to each one. Place the fraction pieces inside labeled envelopes, and post them under the matching circles for students to match up the fractions.

We're Buggy about Insects!

Students will be bugging you to share their insect discoveries on this display. Cover the board with green background paper. Give each student a jar pattern (page 96) to color, cut out, and label with his name. After exploring outside, give students paper to draw and cut out pictures from their insect observations. Glue the students' pictures to the jars and post them on the display. Accent the bulletin board with a border using the elm leaf (page 57) and the bug (page 76) patterns .

Dino-mite Dinosaur Facts!

Relive the dinosaur days. Cover the top half of the board with blue background paper and the bottom half with brown background paper cut to resemble volcanoes. Add lava peaks with red paint or markers. Use an overhead projector to enlarge the pteranodon (page 94), triceratops (page 95), tyrannosaurus (page 95), and apatosaurus (page 96) patterns. Cut out, color, and post the patterns. Copy, color, and cut out the palm tree pattern (page 80) and post along with cotton clouds. Add sentence strips containing dinosaur names and facts.

What's the Weather Like?

See the year's weather at a glance. Cover the board with blue background paper. Make window panes by attaching strips of yellow paper to the board. Use fabric to make curtains to accent the display. Add a wide strip of paper to the bottom to make a windowsill. Label each section of the window with a different season. Copy the raindrop (page 71), cloud (page 71), sun (page 102), and snowflake (page 64) patterns and have students post the appropriate patterns to reflect daily weather conditions.

Observing with Your Five Senses

Tune the class into sights, sounds, and smells. Cover the board with pink paper. Use an overhead projector to enlarge the bug detective pattern (page 102), then color, cut out, and post it on the display. For each magnifying glass, cut two large blue paper circles, one slightly smaller and lighter in shade than the other. Cut a rectangle for each handle and write one of the five senses on each. On a strip of paper, write the name of the object being observed. Inside each magnifying glass, have students write words describing what they see, smell, hear, feel, and taste. Change the display by replacing the inside circle on each magnifying glass and the object name in the title.

Scientists . . .

Explore the world of a scientist with this reference bulletin board. Cover the board with yellow background paper. Use an overhead projector to enlarge the scientist pattern (page 98). Color, cut out, and attach the pattern to the center of the board. Provide students with sentence strips to write the things a scientist does. Let students draw and cut out illustrations for each statement. Post the descriptions and pictures around the scientist.

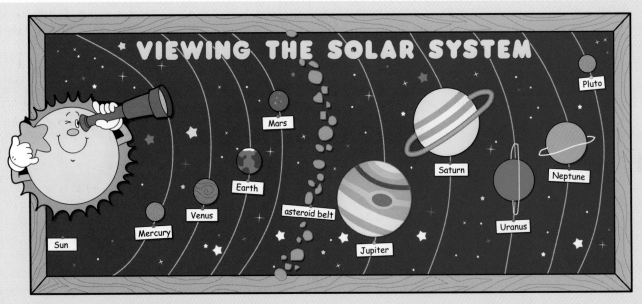

Viewing the Solar System

Young stargazers will love viewing the solar system. Cover the board with dark blue paper. Enlarge, color, and cut out the sun with telescope pattern (page 97). Post the sun on the left edge of the board. Cut various sizes of circles and color them to represent each of the nine planets. Attach the planets to the display and label each. Show their orbits by drawing the path with chalk. Create an asteroid belt by tearing paper shapes and attaching them in a line across the board. Accent the display with gold foil stars.

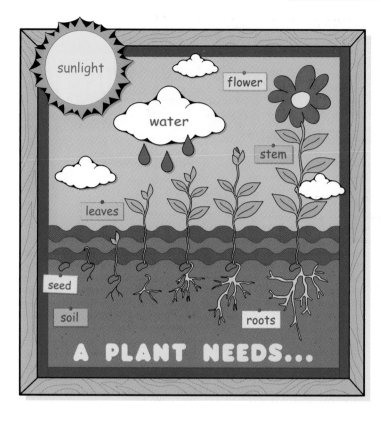

A Plant Needs . . .

How does your garden grow? With sunlight, water, and soil as this display will show! Cover the top half of the display with blue background paper and the bottom half with brown background paper cut to resemble the mounds of soil in a garden. Enlarge, color, cut out, and post copies the cloud (page 71) and raindrop (page 71) patterns , and one copy of the sun pattern (page 102). Have students draw the stages of growth in a plant from seed to flower. Complete the display by labeling each plant part and the things it needs to grow.

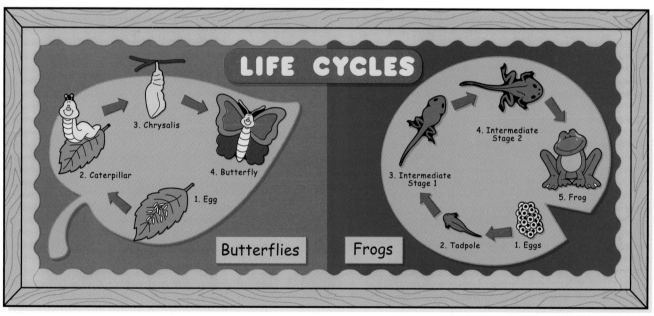

Life Cycles

Illustrate the circle of life. Cover one side of the board with green background paper and the other side with blue background paper. Cut out a large lily pad and a large leaf from green paper and attach them to the display. Enlarge, color, and cut out the following patterns: sitting frog (page 68), frog eggs (page 96), froglet (page 99), tadpole (page 99), tadpole with legs (page 99), butterfly (page 79), caterpillar on leaf (page 98), chrysalis (page 98), and butterfly eggs on leaf (page 99). Post each set of patterns in a circle on the appropriate habitat, labeling and drawing arrows between each stage. Label the sides "Butterflies" and "Frogs."

Our Family Portraits

Put students' picture-perfect families on display. Cover the board with pink background paper. Provide each student with a sheet of colored paper and several copies of the paper doll pattern (page 54) in various sizes. Let students decorate the patterns to resemble each of their family members then glue the patterns to the colored paper. Students can make their pets with construction paper. Have students create frames by gluing paper strips around the edges of their pictures. Accent the frames using glitter and buttons. Hang each picture on the board with a length of yarn and a thumbtack.

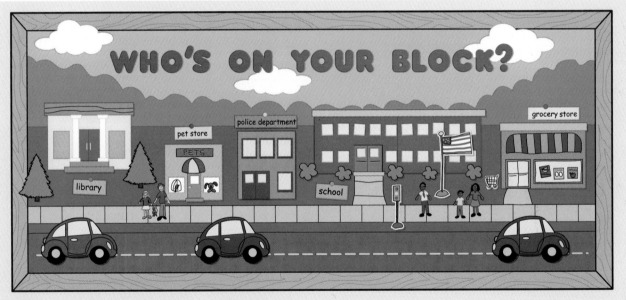

Who's on Your Block?

Who are your school neighbors? Cover the top third of the board with blue background paper and the middle third with green background paper cut to resemble grass and a tree line. At the bottom, add two strips of gray paper marked with lines to resemble a sidewalk and a street. Provide students with paper to color, cut out, and label the buildings, people, and sights on the display. Accent the bulletin board by adding copies of the evergreen tree (page 62) and car (page 103) patterns.

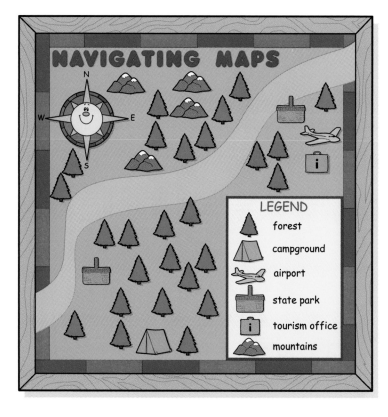

Navigating Maps

Chart a trail for adventure. Cover the board with green background paper. Cut a large strip of blue paper and attach it across the center of the board to resemble a river. Enlarge, color, cut out, and post a copy of the compass rose pattern (page 101). Add a map legend by sizing and gluing the following patterns to a sheet of paper: evergreen tree (page 62) , picnic basket (page 78), tent (page 100), mountains (page 101), airplane (page 105), and suitcase (page 105). Use extra pattern copies to plot areas on the map. Make a border using red and blue paper strips. Write and display questions on index cards for the children to answer.

Ways to Travel!

Keep students moving! Cover the top half of the display with blue background paper and the bottom half with green background paper. Attach blue scalloped paper strips to resemble ocean waves. Cut a strip of gray paper with small strips of yellow paper glued to the middle and attach it to the middle of the board to resemble a road. Enlarge, color, and cut out the following patterns: sailboat (page 80) car (page 103), cruise ship (page 103), train car (page 104), train engine (page 104), and airplane (page 105). Attach the patterns to the appropriate places on the board. Encourage students to draw additional modes of transportation in the sky, on the water, and on land.

When I Grow Up, I Want to Be . . .

Focus on the future with this career display. Cover the board with pink background paper. Give each student a copy of the paper doll pattern (page 54). Have students decorate the patterns to resemble their desired careers. Let each child write about her career and why it interests her. Post the patterns on the display. Cut out a white paper thought balloon to highlight the bulletin board title. Create a border by writing the names of various careers on colored paper rectangles then posting them along the edges of the board.

Who Lives on the Farm?

Farm fun has begun! Cover the top quarter of the board with blue paper and the bottom three-fourths with green paper cut to resemble rolling hills. Add paper clouds and a sunrise. Enlarge, color, cut out, and post the barn (page 72) and boy on tractor (page 106) patterns. Cut out the space above the barn doors. Cut between the barn doors and fold them back. Let students draw and cut out animals to display in the barns labeled with animal names. Add sheep by gluing cotton and black paper pieces to plain paper.

"Beary" Interesting News

Let this beary clever display keep your class posted. Cover the board with newspaper. Enlarge the bear left foot, bear left paw, bear right foot, bear right paw, and bear head patterns (page 106-107). Color and cut out the patterns. Attach a piece of poster board to the center of the display. Arrange the bear around the poster board. Cut out interesting local and national news articles and display them on the poster board. Accent the display by rolling sheets of newspaper and attaching them to the edges of the board.

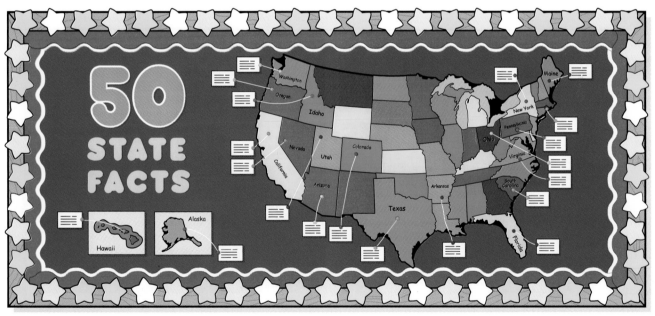

50 State Facts

Travel across the United States in search of fifty fun facts. Cover the display with dark blue background paper. Enlarge the Alaska, Hawaii, and continental U.S. patterns (pages 107-108) using an overhead projector. Let students color the patterns, then post them on the board. Label each state. Have students research and write facts about each state on an index card. Post the cards on the board and connect them to the appropriate states using lengths of yarn and thumbtacks. Complete the bulletin board by making a border using copies of the star pattern (page 85).

Special Recognition

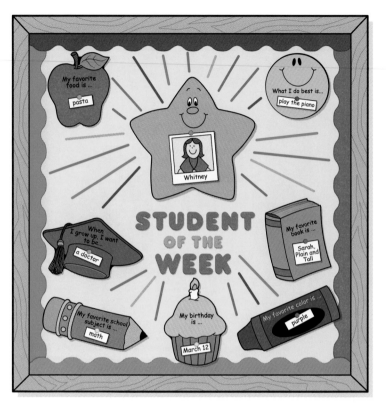

Student of the Week

Shine the spotlight on students. Cover the board with yellow background paper. Enlarge the star with face pattern (page 85). Then, color, cut out, and attach it to the center of the board. Post a labeled photograph of the student in the middle of the star. Personalize the display for each star student by attaching colored copies of the following patterns: apple (page 52), pencil (page 84), smiley face (page 91), book (page 109), cupcake (page 110), crayon (page 110), and graduation cap (page 111). Label each pattern with statements for the student to answer on paper strips.

I'm Special Because . . .

Give students special recognition. Cover the board with blue background paper. Make trophy shelves by attaching long strips of paper around the edges of the board and across the middle. Decorate a yellow paper rectangle to resemble an award plaque and write the display title inside. Give each student a copy of the trophy pattern (page 109) to color and cut out. Have each student personalize his trophy then write something that makes him special on the star. Display the trophies on the trophy shelves.

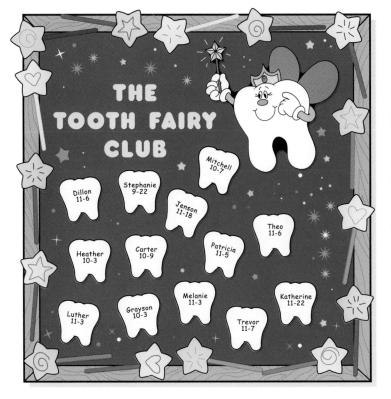

The Tooth Fairy Club

Big smiles are sure to abound when students see their names on this display. Cover the board with dark blue background paper. Enlarge, color, and cut out the Tooth Fairy pattern (page 111) and attach it to the board. Copy and cut out several copies of the tooth pattern (page 110). When a student loses a tooth, write her name and the date on a tooth pattern, then post it on the display. Have students make fairy wands by decorating copies of the star pattern (page 85) and attaching colored dowel rods or straws to each. Accent the board with the fairy wands.

Happy Birthday to You!

Extend happy birthday wishes to your students with this festive display. Cover the board with pink background paper or wrapping paper. Make a large bow using paper, ribbon, or fabric and attach it to the corner of the board so the board resembles a gift box. Enlarge a class supply of candle patterns (pages 60) and twelve cake patterns (page 112). Color and cut out the patterns. Label each cake with the name of a month. Post the cakes on the display. Write each student's name and birth date on a candle pattern, then place the candles on the appropriate cake.

The Friend"ship"

Set sail for a friendly voyage. Cover the top three-fourths of the board with light blue background paper. Cover the bottom fourth of the board with layered strips of blue scalloped paper to resemble ocean waves. Accent the scene with paper clouds and a sunset. Use an overhead projector to enlarge the flagship pattern (page 115). Have each student draw his self-portrait on the sail. Cut out and attach the ship to the middle of the board. Provide paper strips for students to write the traits of a good friend to display on the board. Accent the scene using the seagull pattern (page 114).

Beaming with Pride

Brighten the classroom! Cover the top two-thirds of the board with dark blue background paper. Create an ocean by layering blue scalloped paper border on the bottom third of the board. Add a strip of brown paper to resemble a beach. Create a fence by attaching semicircles and rectangles cut from brown paper. Connect the fence with yellow yarn. Enlarge, color, cut out, and post the lighthouse pattern (page 114). Create light beams by cutting large triangles from yellow paper. Write class achievements on the beams.

Read and Succeed!

Show "whoo" loves to read. Cover the display with yellow background paper. Enlarge, color, and cut out the owl with books pattern (page 113) and post it in the corner of the display. Make several copies of the book stack pattern (page 112). Color and cut out the patterns, and layer them to create a large book stack. Write individual goals for the number of books students need to read on the spines of the books. Copy, color, cut out, and write the class reading goal on the baby mouse pattern (page 113). Post the mouse on top of the stack of books. Write each child's name on a paper strip and move it up as she reads more books.

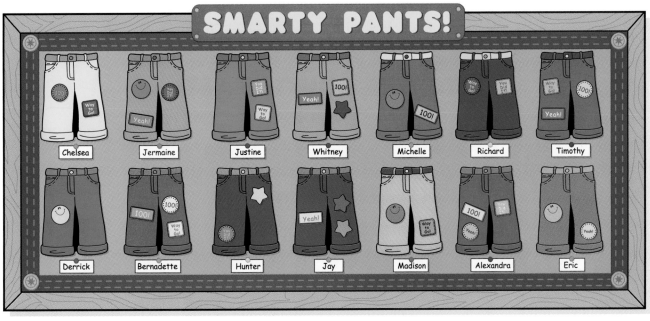

Smarty Pants!

Fashion a fun reward display! Cover the display with bright green background paper. Give each student a copy of the pants pattern (page 116) to color and cut out. Post the patterns on the board with student names written on paper strips, which are attached below them. Reward students by giving them copies of the patch 1, patch 2, and patch 3 (pages 116–117), star (page 85), and the smiley face (page 91) patterns (after writing positive phrases to them). Have students place the patches on their pants. Accent the display with a denim border made from blue paper strips with stitch marks drawn with light blue chalk and jean rivets cut from orange paper.

Building Good Character

Reinforce character building blocks . Cover the top third of the board with light blue paper. Cover the bottom two-thirds of the board with brown paper cut to resemble a beach. Accent the scene with ocean waves made from blue paper scalloped strips and an orange paper sun and white paper clouds. Enlarge, color, cut out, and post the beach mouse pattern (page 118). On sheets of brown paper, write examples of good character, then post in the shape of a sand castle, adding paper flags to the top. Complete with the sand dollar, shell 1, and shell 2 (pages 118 and 121) patterns.

Be a Teacher's Pet . . .

Every student is a favorite with this idea. Cover the board with yellow background paper. Give students copies of the cat (page 120) or dog (page 121) pattern to color and cut out. Write each student's name on a paper strip. On the back of the strip, attach a loop of yarn. Post the papers under each child's pattern. Each time a student completes his homework, add a pet collar (paper loop) to his name strip. Accent the display with copies of the bone (pages 56) and paw print (page 120) patterns.

Blue-Ribbon Behavior

Reward your students' first-rate behavior with this shining display. Cover the board with blue background paper. Use an overhead projector to enlarge the trophy pattern (page 109), then color, cut out, and post it. Enlarge, color, and cut out a copy of the award ribbon pattern (page 117). Write a positive phrase on the award ribbon and place it beside the trophy. Give each student a copy of the award ribbon pattern to color, cut out, and personalize with their names, then post for the border. Place gold stars on their ribbons to acknowledge good behavior. Accent the display with colored copies of the star pattern (page 85).

Serving Up Good Behavior

Give your class a helping of positive reinforcement with this display idea. Cover the board with red background paper. Enlarge the elephant cook pattern (page 119) using an overhead projector. Color, cut out, and attach the pattern to the right side of the display. Make an "Order Here" sign with a strip of paper. Give each student a copy of the french fry box pattern (page 119) to color, cut out, and personalize with her name. Use painted craft sticks or paper strips to represent french fries. When a student demonstrates good behavior, place a french fry in his container. Add strips of paper cut with a scalloped edge to complete the bulletin board.

We Don't Clown Around...

Students will jump through hoops to help with this display idea. Cover the board with orange background paper. Enlarge copies of the clown pattern (page 123). Color, cut out, and label each pattern with a classroom job. Enlarge, color, and cut out a class supply of the balloon 1 (page 120) and balloon 2 (page 121) patterns. Write a student's name on each balloon pattern. Attach the clowns to the display. Assign classroom jobs by placing the balloons beside the clowns, using lengths of string to connect them. Create a border by cutting out various-sized circles to surround the display.

We're Doing a Whale of a Job!

Swim in a sea of great helpers with this bulletin board. Cover the top quarter of the board with light blue background paper. Cut strips of dark blue background paper to resemble ocean waves to cover the rest of the board. Accent the display by adding cotton clouds. Enlarge the whale and water spray patterns (page 122). On each whale pattern, write a classroom job. Write students' names on the water spray patterns. Assign jobs by placing a water spray above each whale.

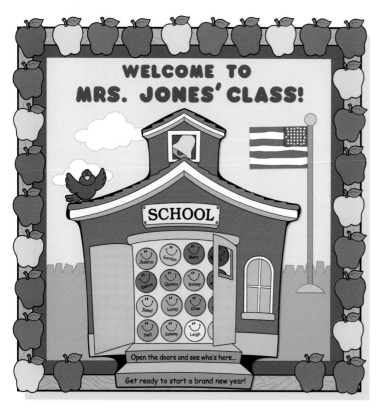

Welcome to Our Class!

Welcome your class with open doors. Cover the top half of the board with blue background paper. Cover the bottom half with green paper cut to resemble grass. Use an overhead projector to enlarge the schoolhouse pattern (page 86). Then, color and cut it. Cut around the schoolhouse doors so that they open. Post the schoolhouse with a copy of the bird pattern (page 68) resting on the roof. Draw a flagpole. Make copies of the smiley face pattern (page 91) to color, cut out, and personalize with students' names. Attach the smiley faces inside the schoolhouse doors. Create a border using the apple pattern (page 52).

We All Share the Load!

Everyone can carry their weight. Cover the top quarter of the board with blue background paper. Cover the bottom three-quarters of the board with green background paper cut to resemble grass. Copy, color, and cut out the sun (page 102) and cloud (page 71) patterns. Add flowers made from tissue paper and chenille craft sticks. Enlarge, color, cut out, and post ant 1, ant 2, and ant 3 patterns (pages 76-78). Enlarge the following patterns: pie (page 50), apple (pages 52), pear (pages 52), carrot (page 73), and watermelon (page 124). Color, cut out, and write a job on each pattern and post above each ant. Write students' names on paper strips and assign jobs weekly.

Get on Board for First Grade!

Cruise into a great year with this display. Cover the board with blue background paper. Cut out and post paper clouds. Add a strip of black paper dashed with yellow paper strips to the bottom of the board to resemble a street. Use an overhead projector to enlarge the bus pattern (page 125). Color and cut out the bus. Have students draw self-portraits inside the bus windows. Draw a picture of yourself in the bus driver's seat. Cut out the bus and post it on the display.

A Good Listener . . .

Students will get an earful of good listening advice with this reference display. Cover the top two-thirds of the display with pink background paper and the bottom third with blue paper. Enlarge the elephant and cat pattern (page 124) using an overhead projector. Color and cut out the pattern and post it on one side of the display. Cut strips of colored paper that gradually narrow and attach them next to the elephant's ear. On each strip of paper, write a characteristic of a good listener.

We Follow the Rules

Encourage positive behavior with this bulletin board. Cover the board with yellow background paper. Give each child a paper plate to decorate as a self-portrait. Provide buttons, yarn, sequins, and colored paper for the children to make hair and clothing. Post each portrait on the board. Cut large speech balloons from white paper. Inside each speech balloon, have a child write a behavior that demonstrates good character. Then, post the speech balloons beside the portraits. Complete the display by creating a border using the pencil pattern (page 84).

Playground Rules

It's all fun and games for students who follow the rules. Cover the top third of the board with blue background paper. Cover the bottom two-thirds with green background paper. Make a fence by cutting and attaching white paper rectangles to the display. Add paper flowers and clouds. Use an overhead projector to enlarge the sliding dog and slide patterns (page 126). Color, cut out, and post the patterns on the board. Write playground rules on sentence strips, then post them on the display.

Getting to the Core . . .

Show students what they will be learning. Cover the board with blue background paper. Enlarge and copy the apple (page 52), apple core (page 127) and apple with bite (page 127) patterns. Color and cut out the patterns. On each apple leaf, write a school subject. Inside the appropriate apple, write topics the class will be learning about in each subject area. Accent the display with the worm pattern (page 127). Create a border by attaching alternating squares of colored paper to the edges of the display.

Have a Bubbly Good Day!

As students pop in, take attendance. Cover the top half of the board with yellow background paper and the bottom half with purple background paper. Use an overhead projector to enlarge the gum ball machine pattern (page 128). Color, cut out, and post the pattern on the board. Cut out a class supply of paper circles for gum balls. Write student names inside each gum ball and attach them to the board with a thumbtack. As students arrive each day, have them move their gum balls into the gum ball machine.

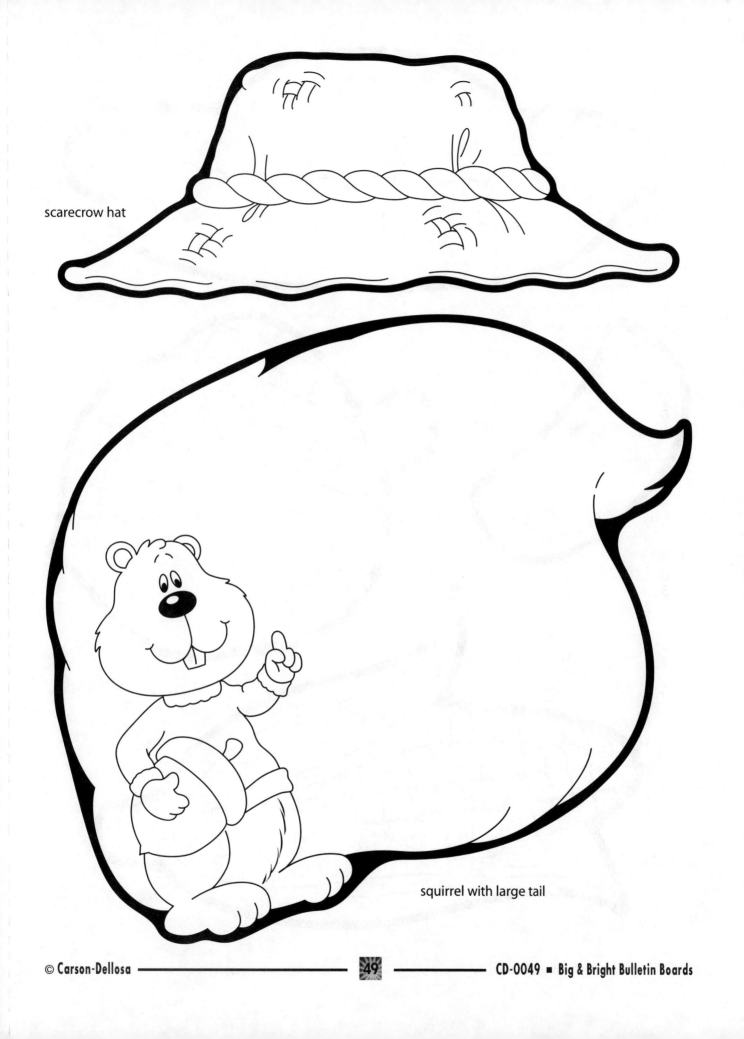

scarecrow hat

squirrel with large tail

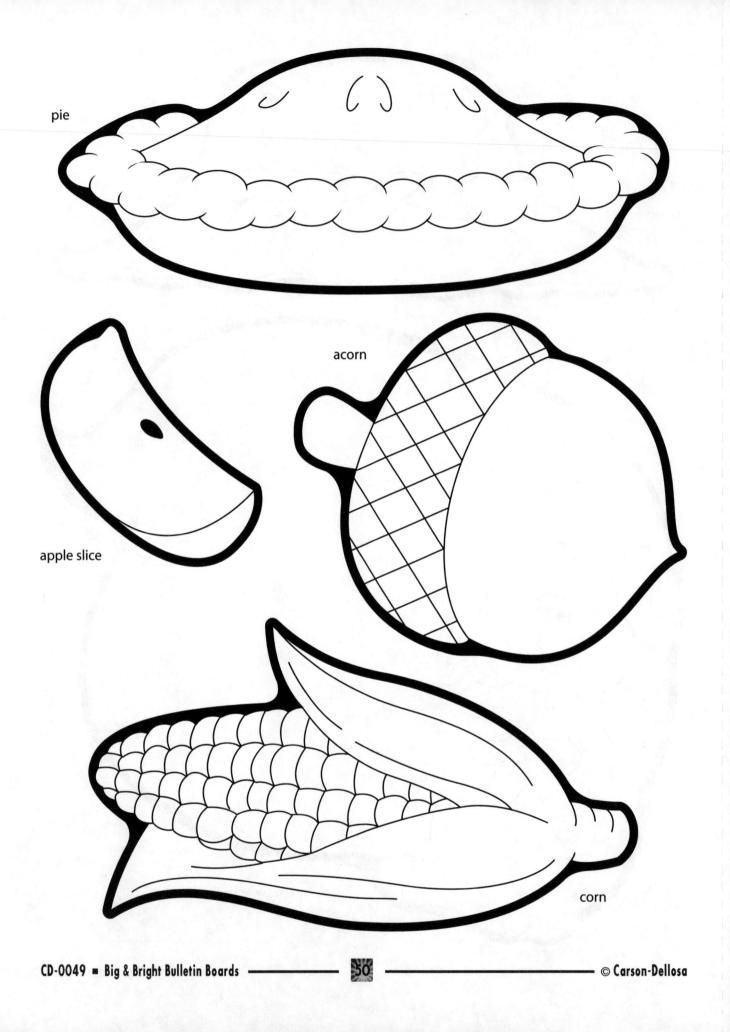

pie

acorn

apple slice

corn

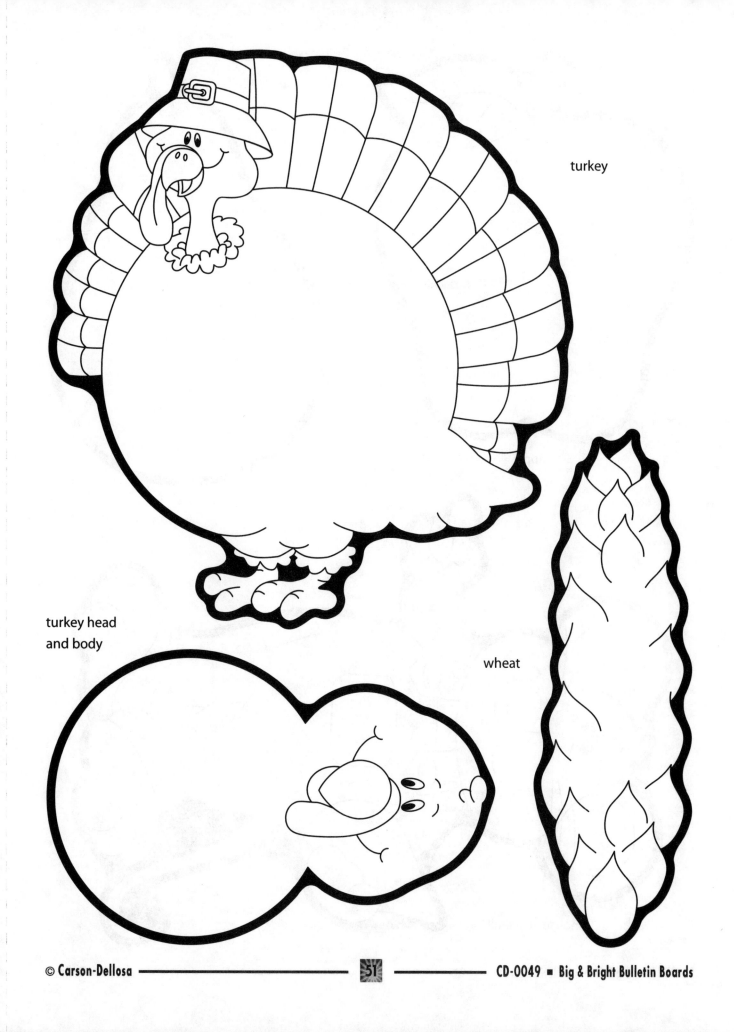

turkey

turkey head
and body

wheat

pear

apple

mouse in overalls

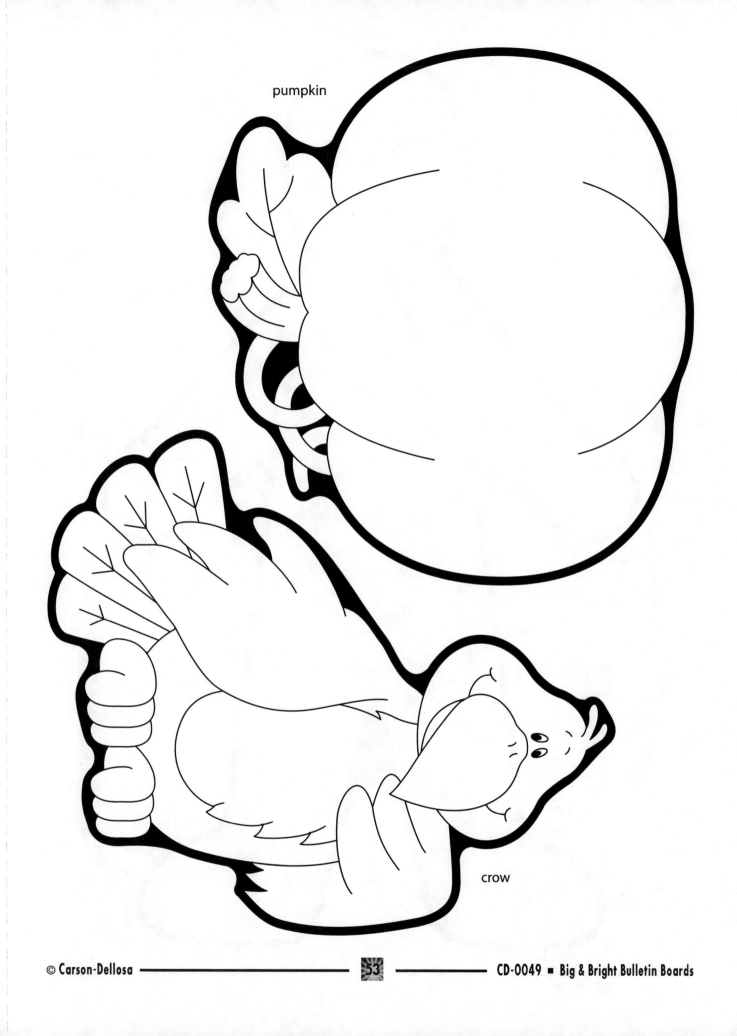

pumpkin

crow

paper doll

bat

happy squirrel

bone

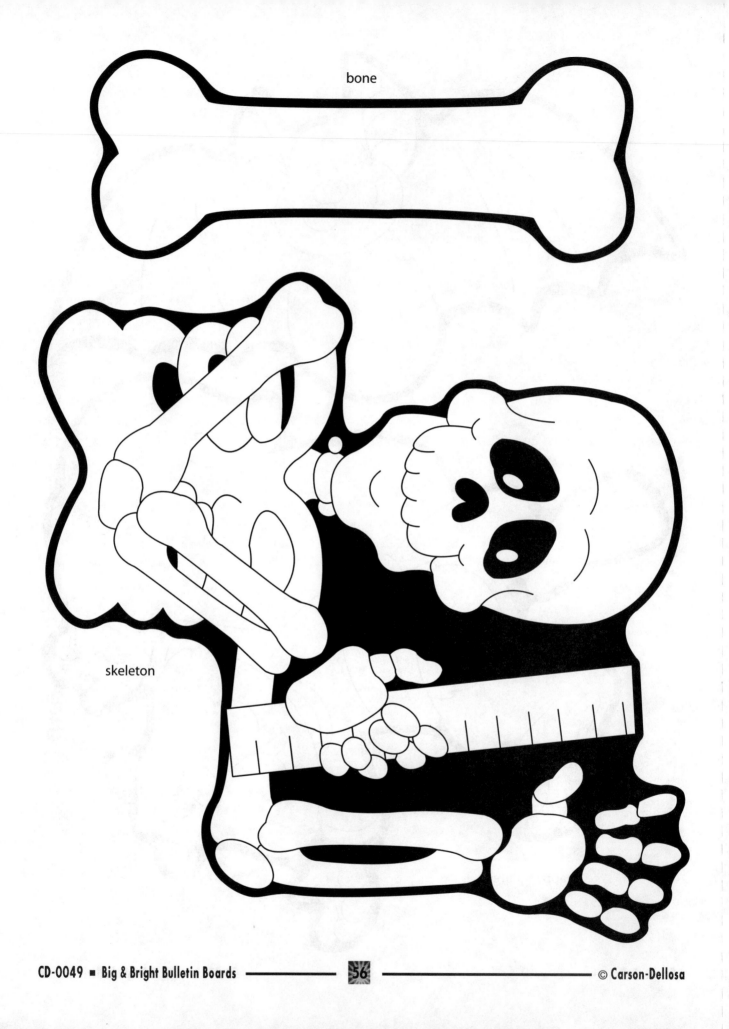

skeleton

oak leaf

aspen leaf

maple leaf

elm leaf

Santa Claus

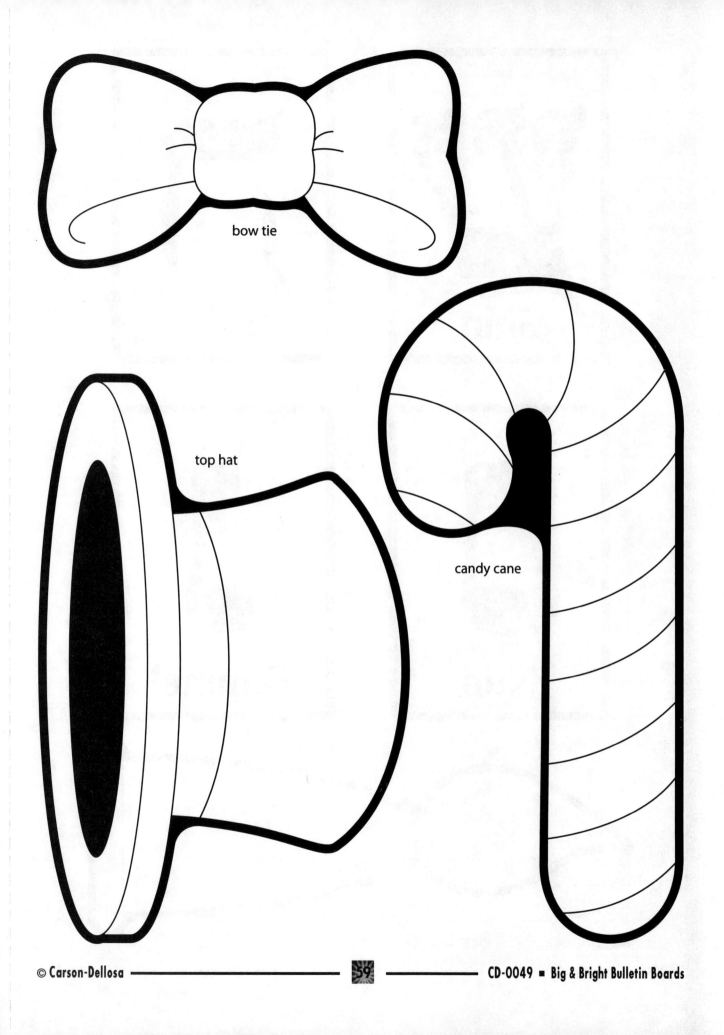

bow tie

top hat

candy cane

Shin

Hey

sides of dreidel

Nun

Gimmel

candle

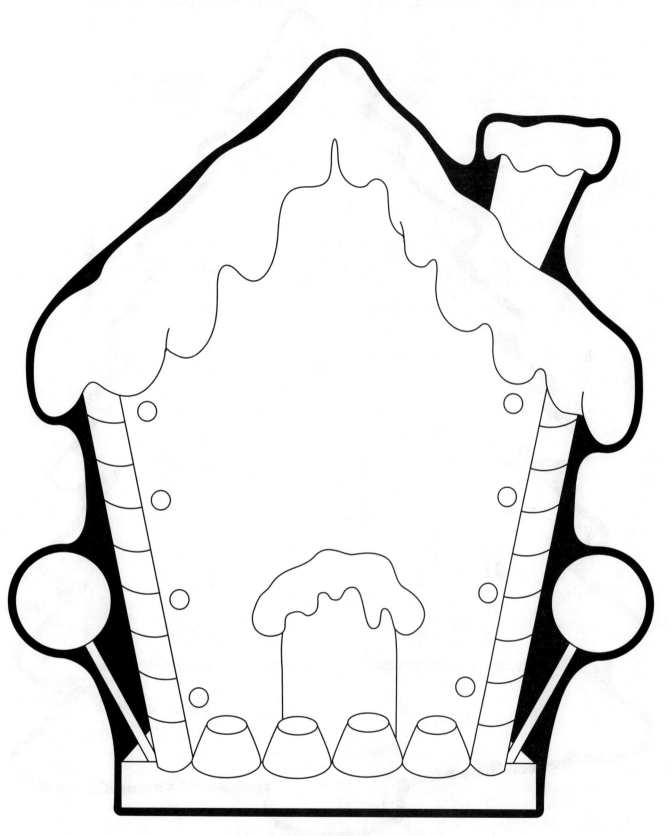

gingerbread house

evergreen tree

Baby New Year

clock

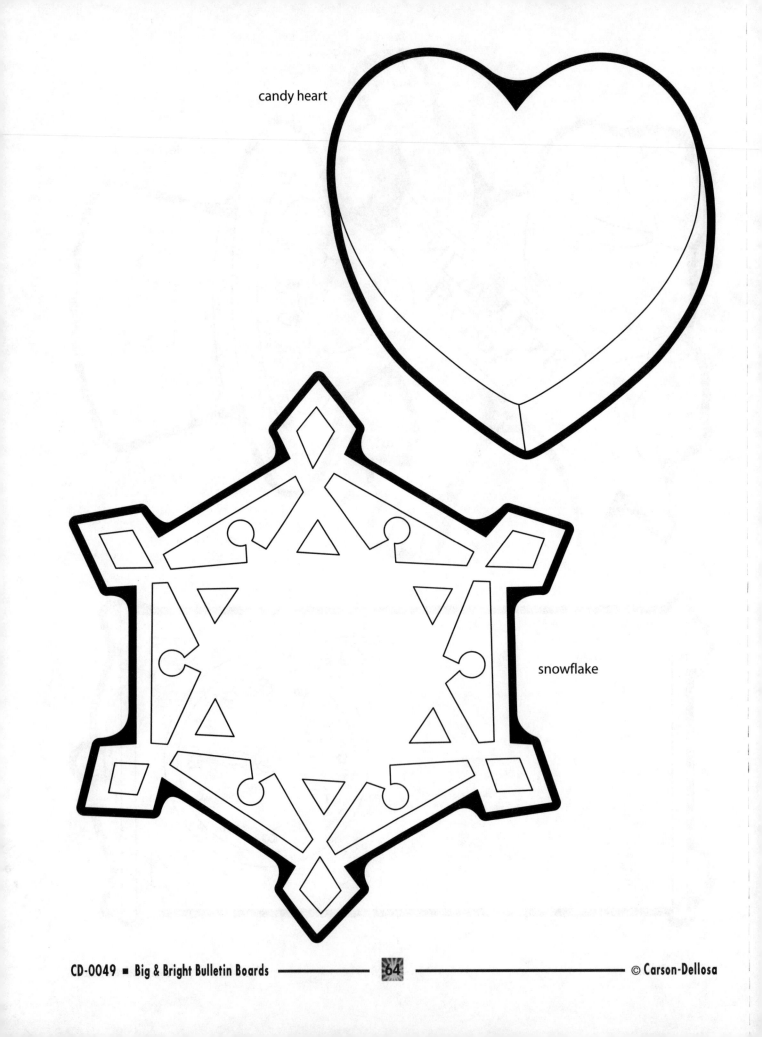

candy heart

snowflake

penguin

valentine bear

BE MINE

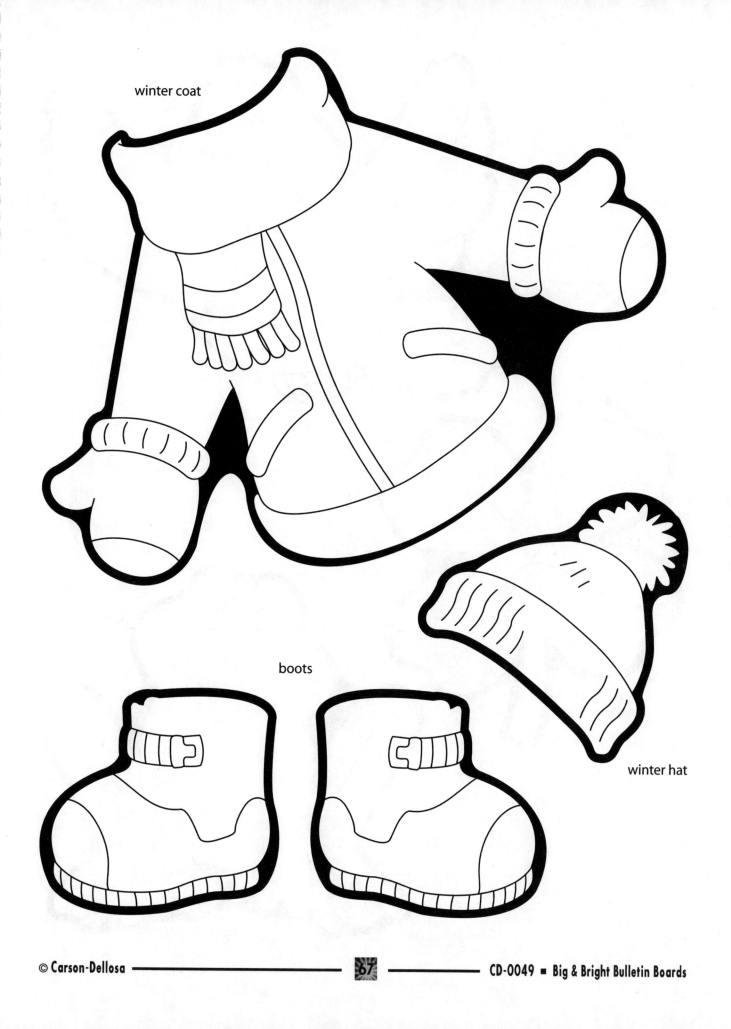

winter coat

boots

winter hat

bird

four-leaf clover

sitting frog

shamrock

turtle with
watering can

leprechaun

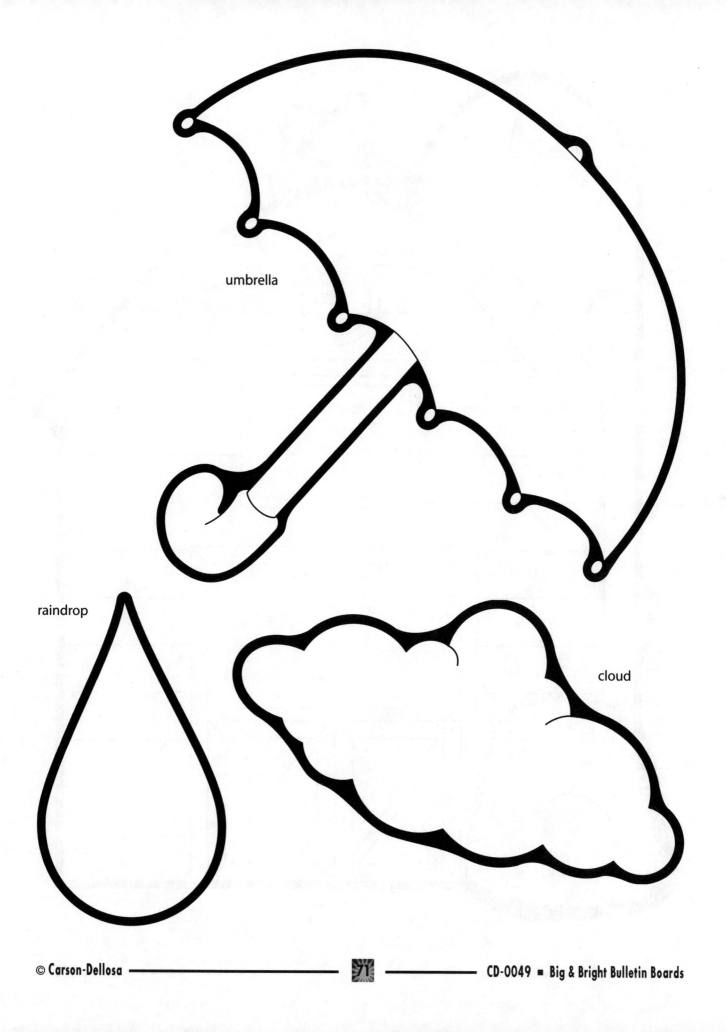

umbrella

raindrop

cloud

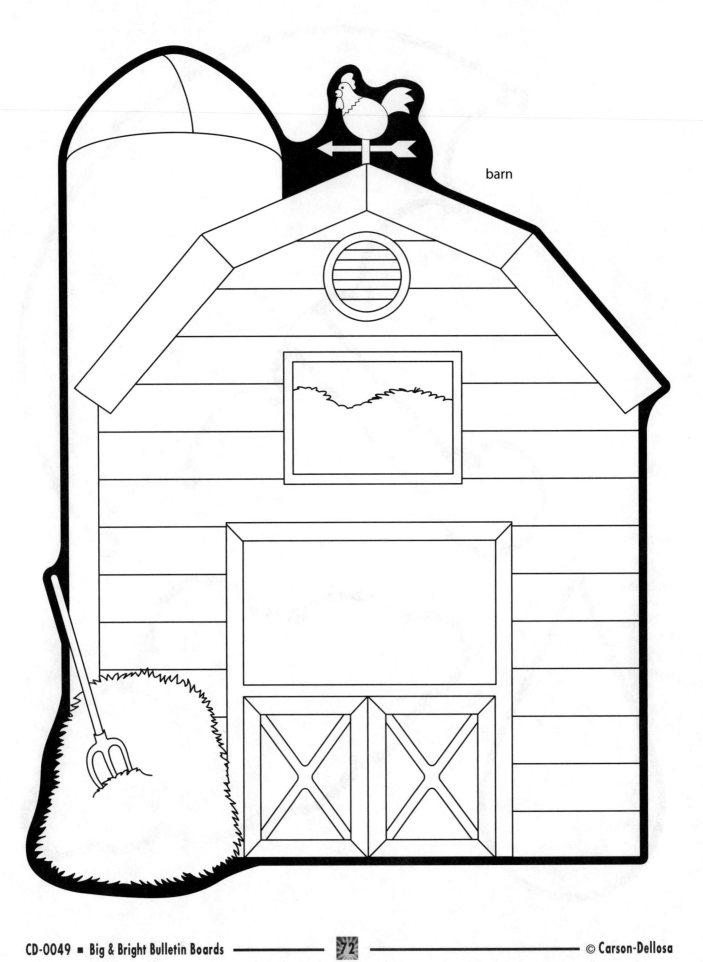

barn

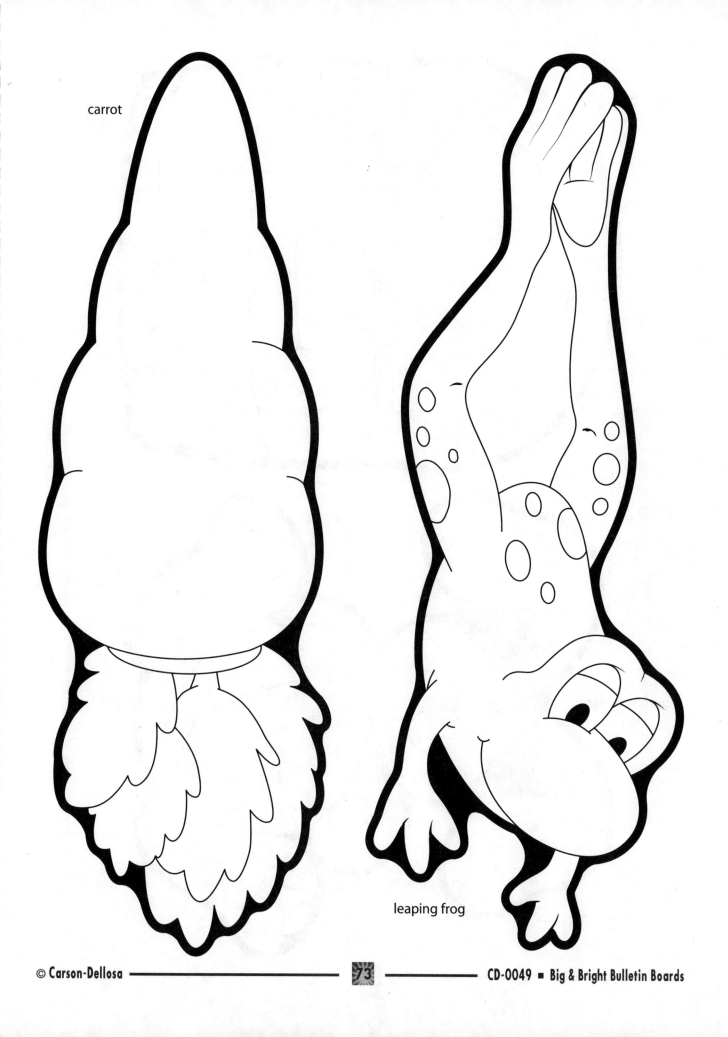

carrot

leaping frog

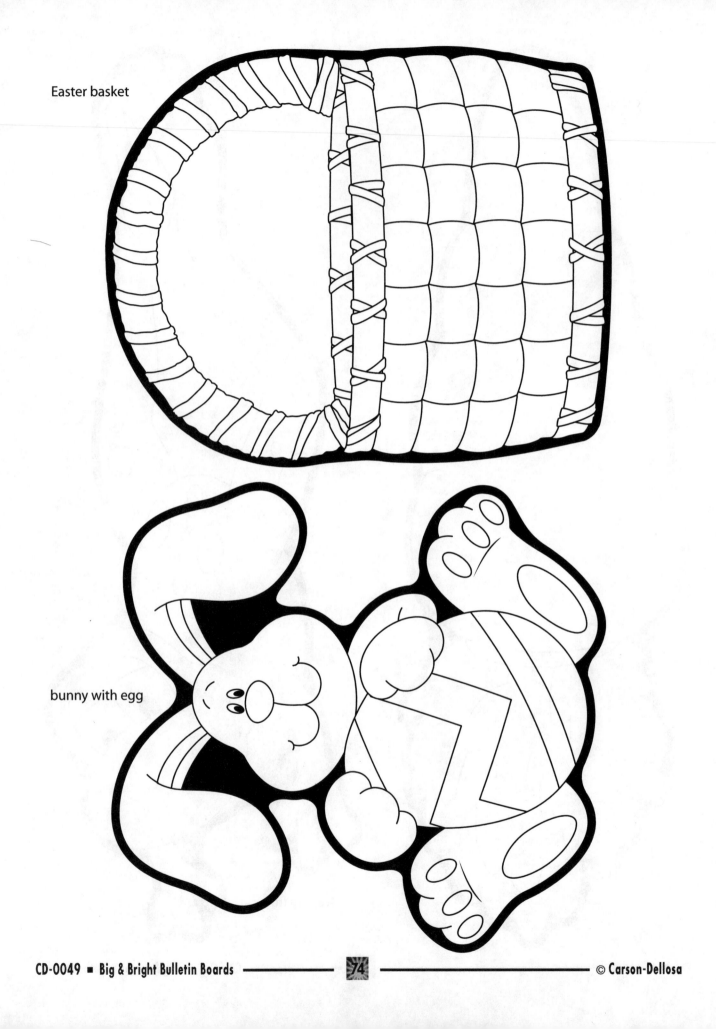

Easter basket

bunny with egg

egg

gardening rabbit

ant 1

bug

ice pop

ant 2

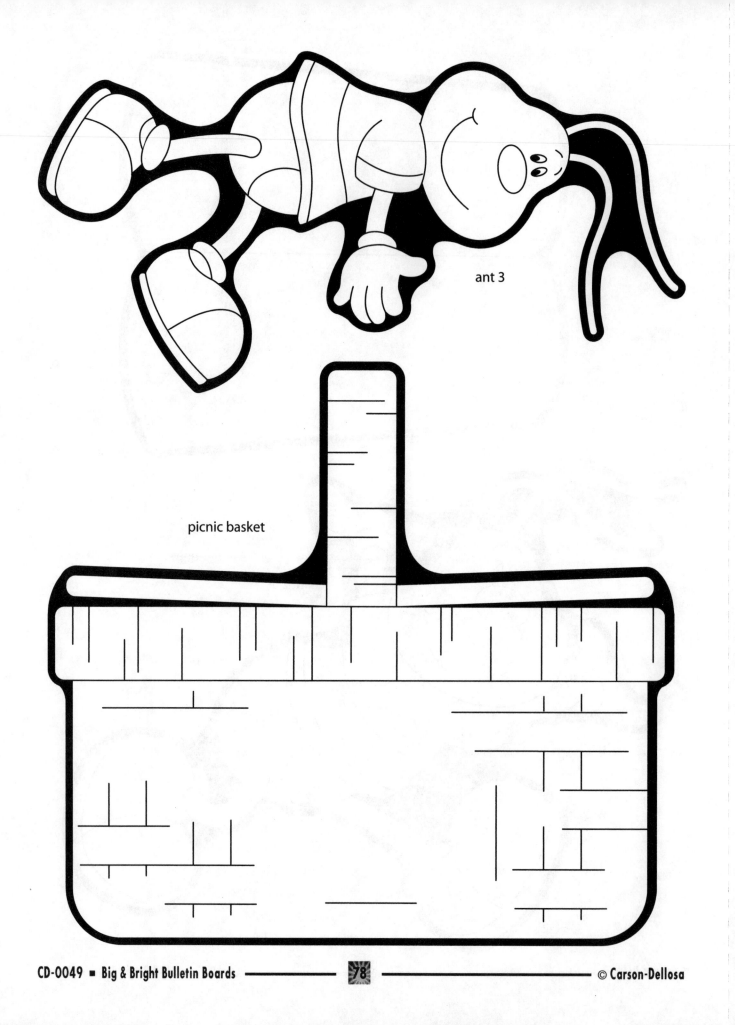

ant 3

picnic basket

butterfly

fish

sailboat

palm tree

graduation ribbon

monkey

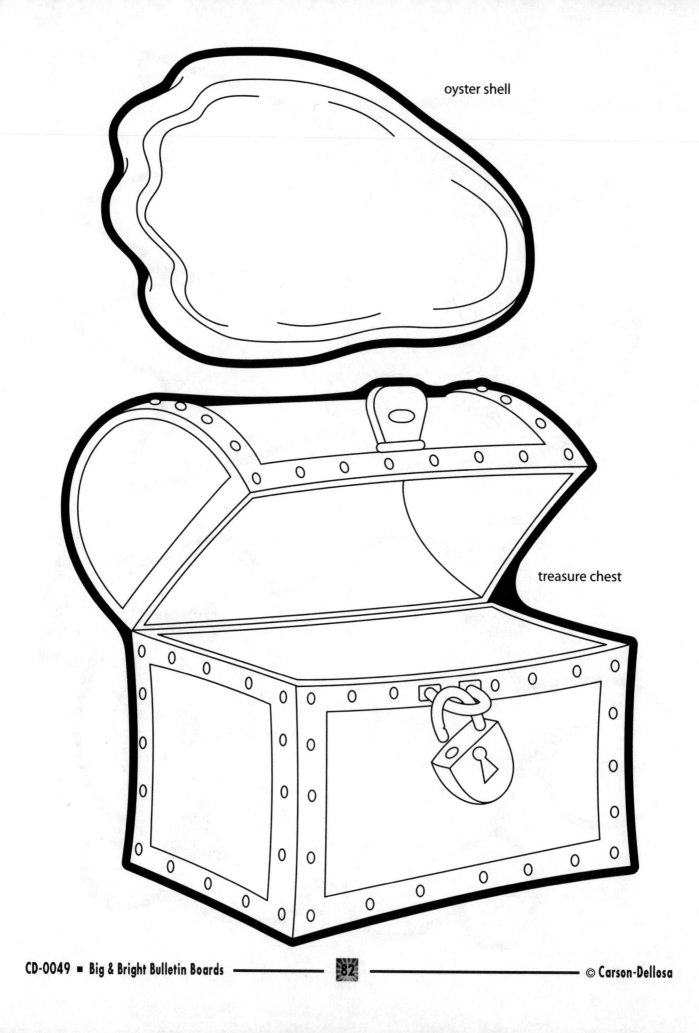

oyster shell

treasure chest

diver

CD-0049 ■ Big & Bright Bulletin Boa

sunglasses

pencil

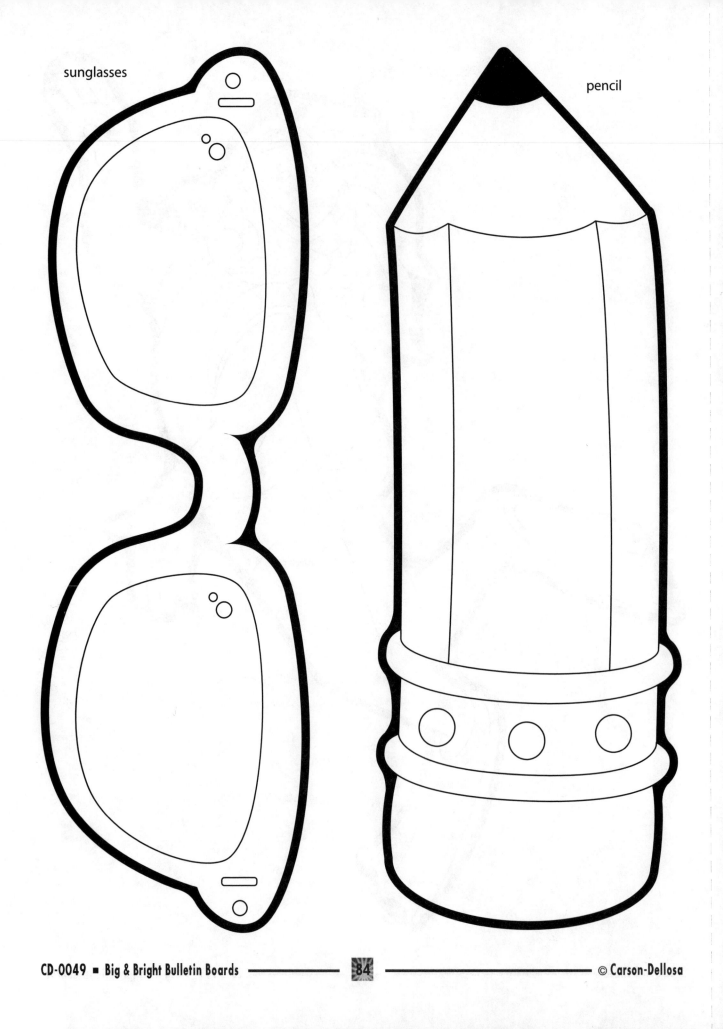

flower

star with face

star

baseball cap

SCHOOL

schoolhouse

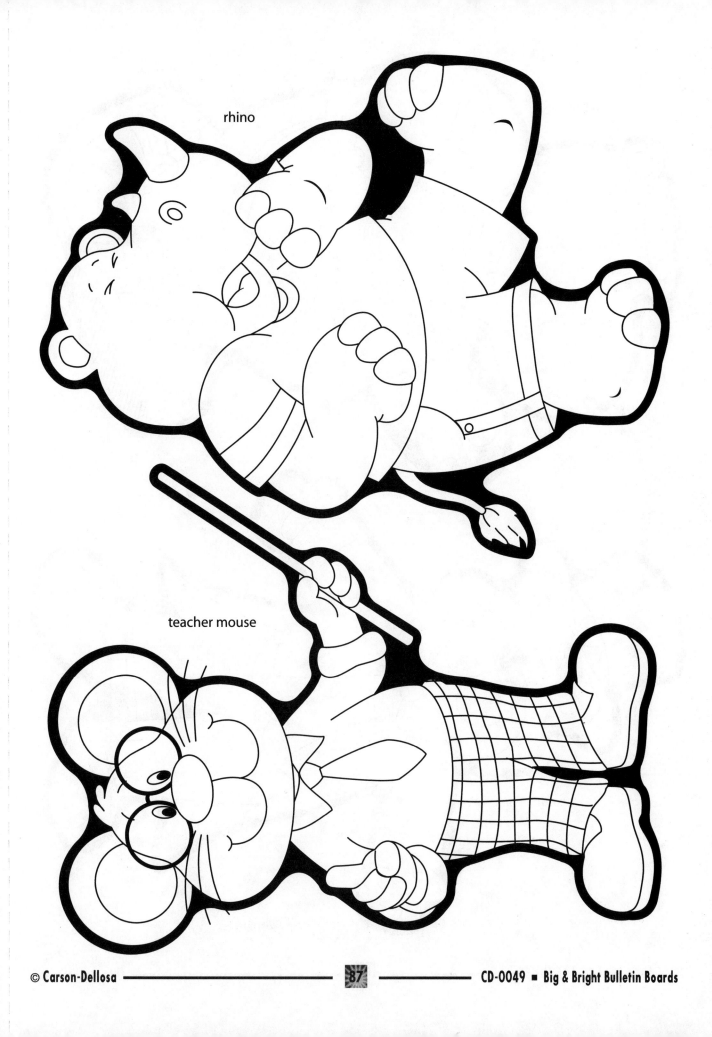

rhino

teacher mouse

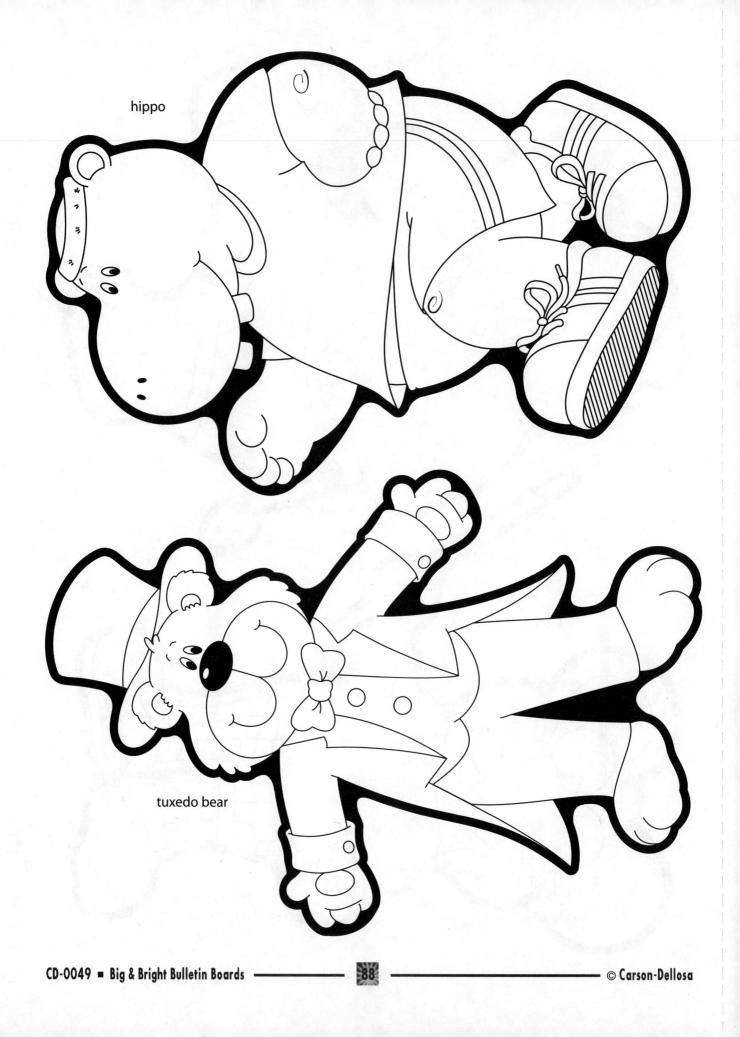

hippo

tuxedo bear

secret agent

file folder

TOP SECRET

ruler with face

boy with sign

smiley face

clock hands

construction mouse

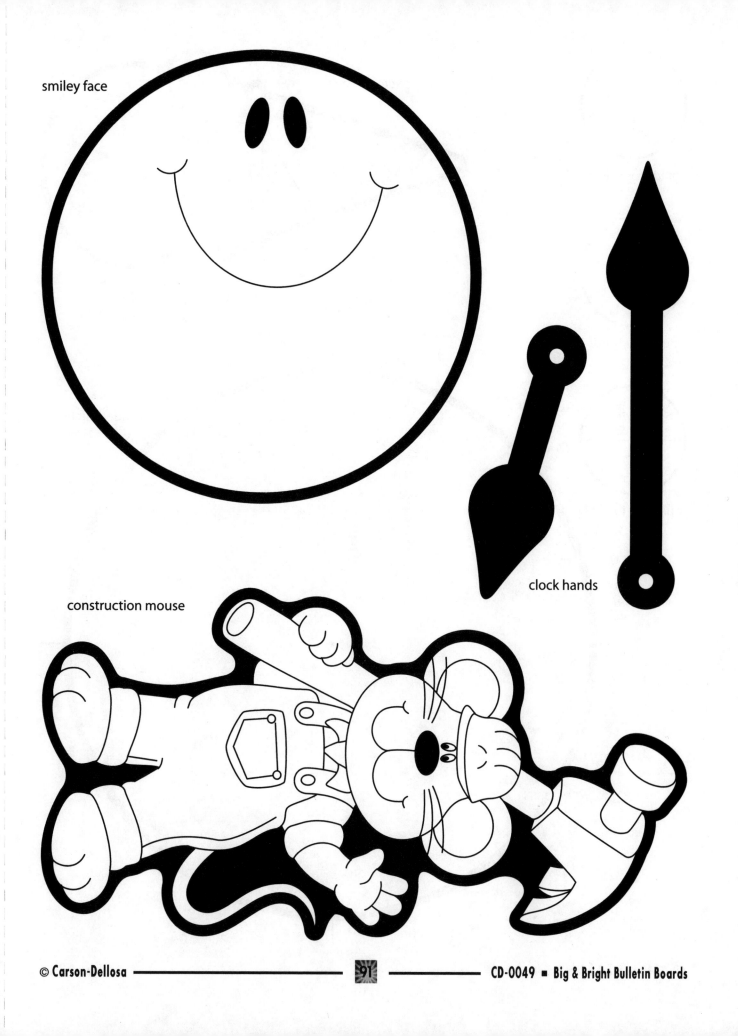

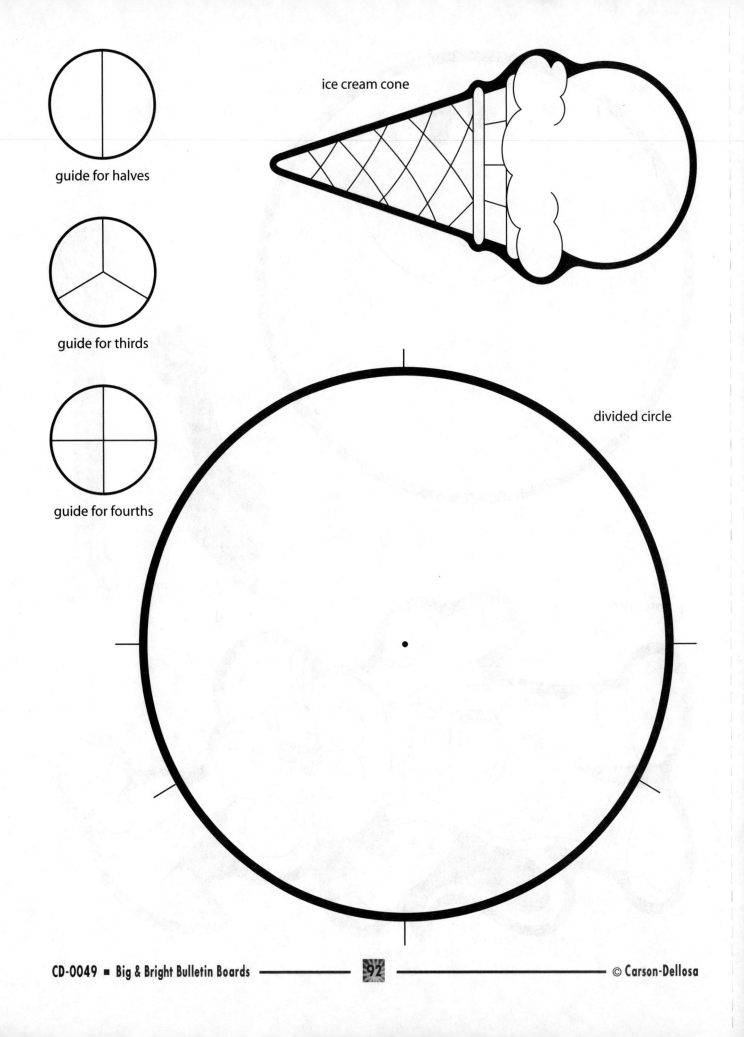

guide for halves

guide for thirds

guide for fourths

ice cream cone

divided circle

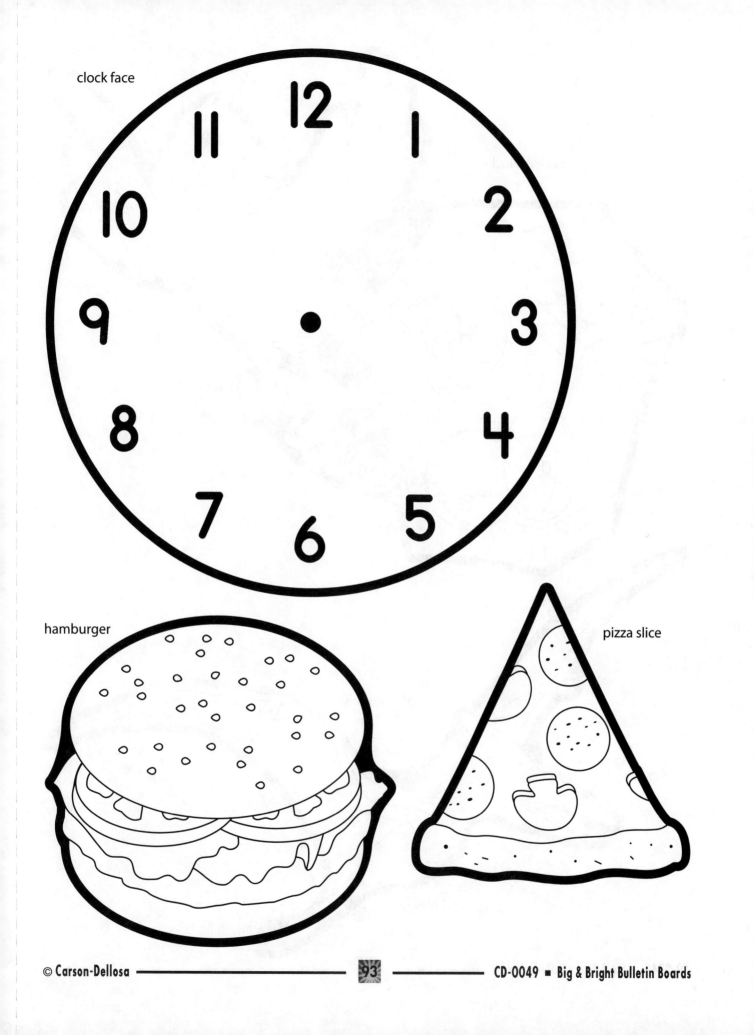

clock face

hamburger

pizza slice

cuckoo clock

pteranodon

tyrannosaurus

triceratops

CD-0049 ■ Big & Bright Bulletin Boards

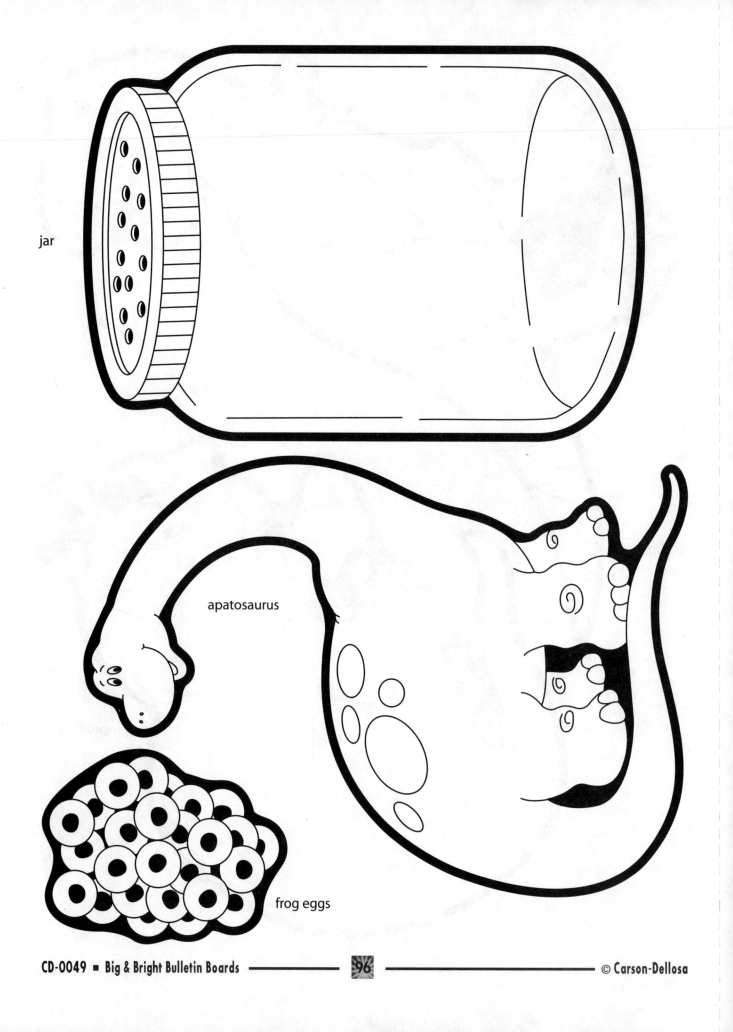

jar

apatosaurus

frog eggs

sun with telescope

chrysalis

scientist

caterpillar on leaf

butterfly eggs on leaf

froglet

tadpole

tadpole with legs

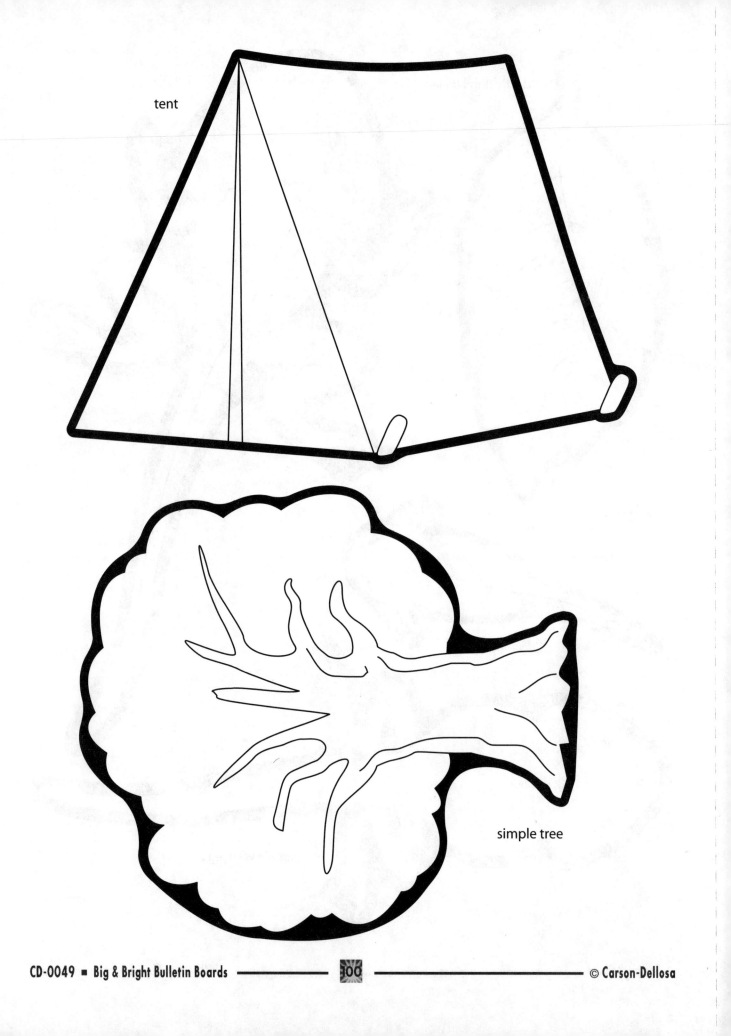

tent

simple tree

compass rose

mountains

bug detective

sun

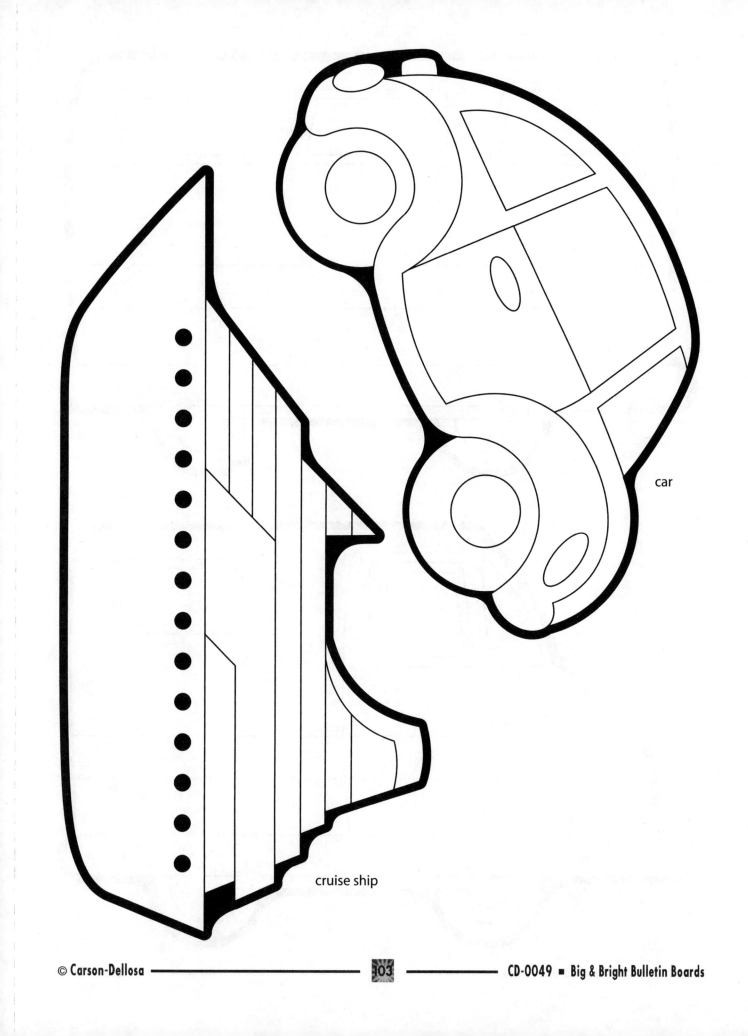

car

cruise ship

train car

train engine

airplane

suitcase

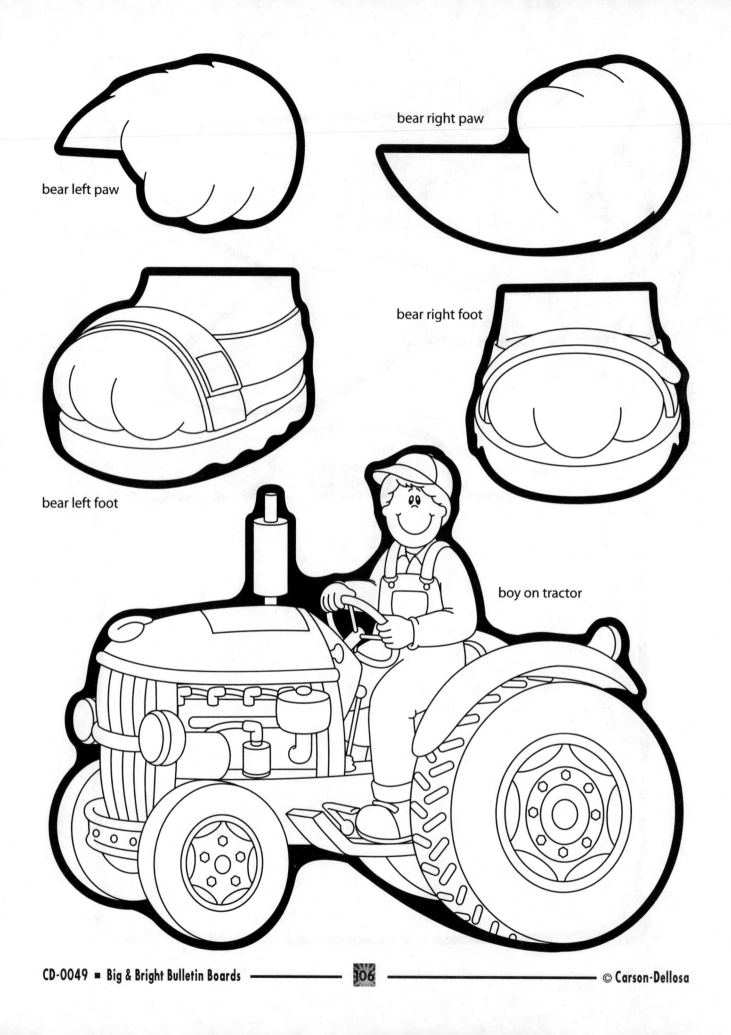

bear left paw

bear right paw

bear left foot

bear right foot

boy on tractor

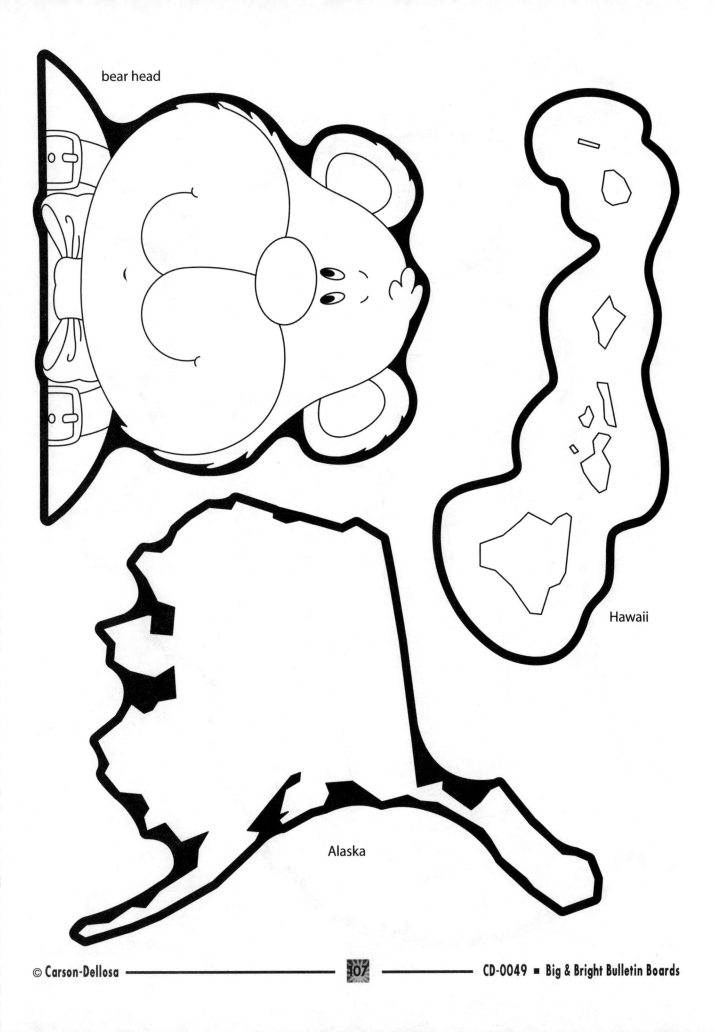

bear head

Hawaii

Alaska

CD-0049 ■ Big & Bright Bulletin Boards

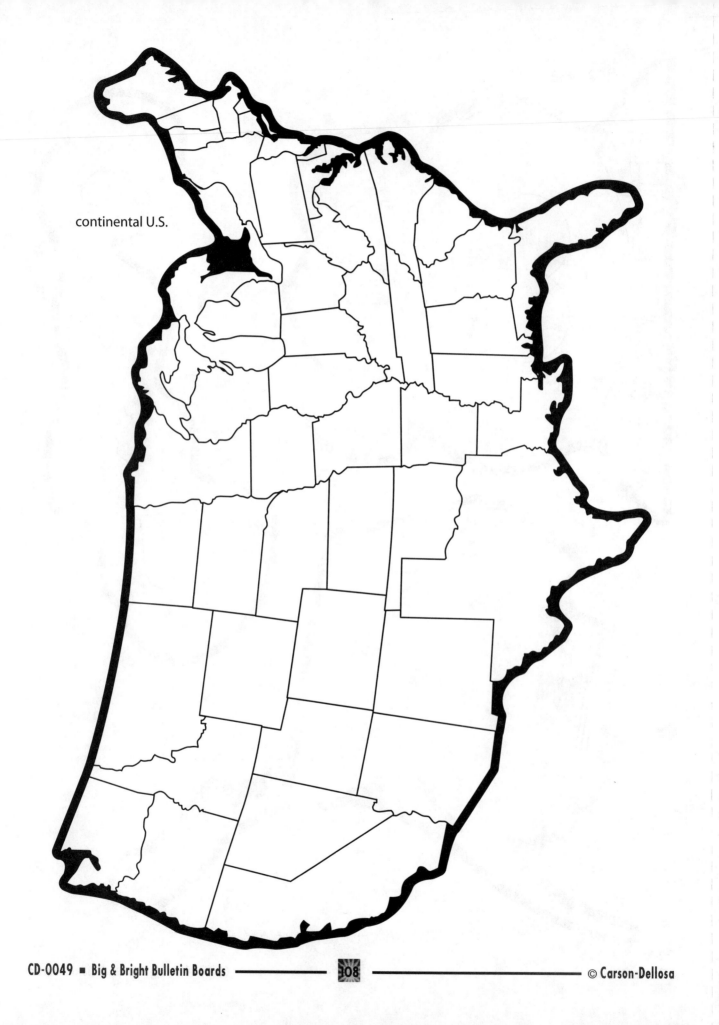

continental U.S.

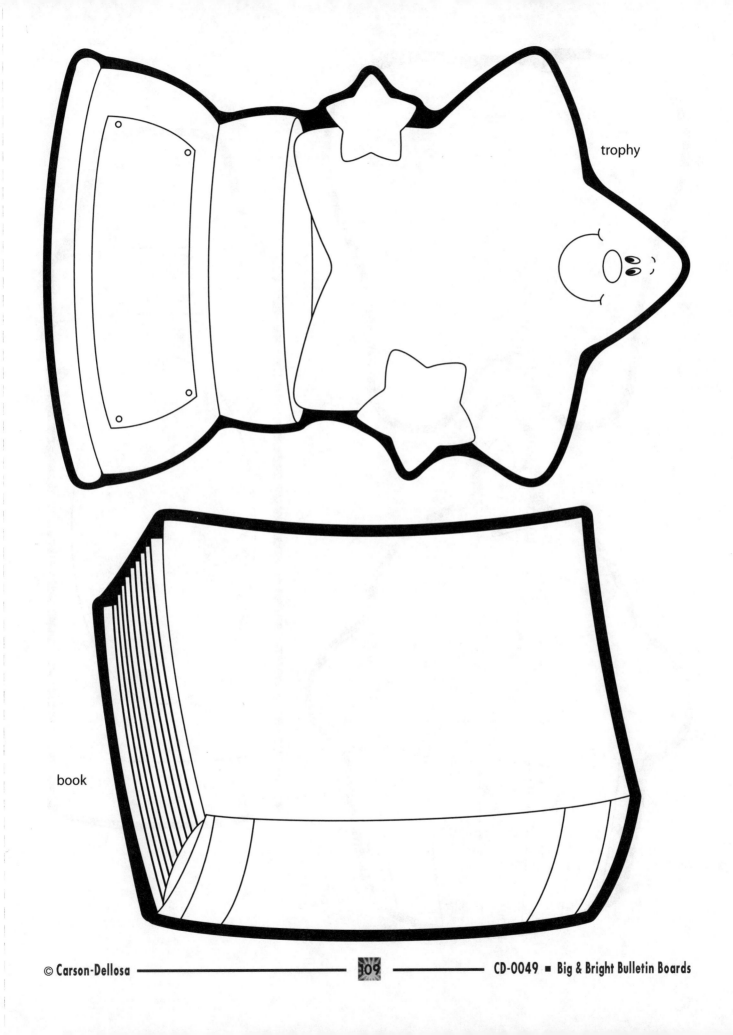

trophy

book

tooth

cupcake

crayon

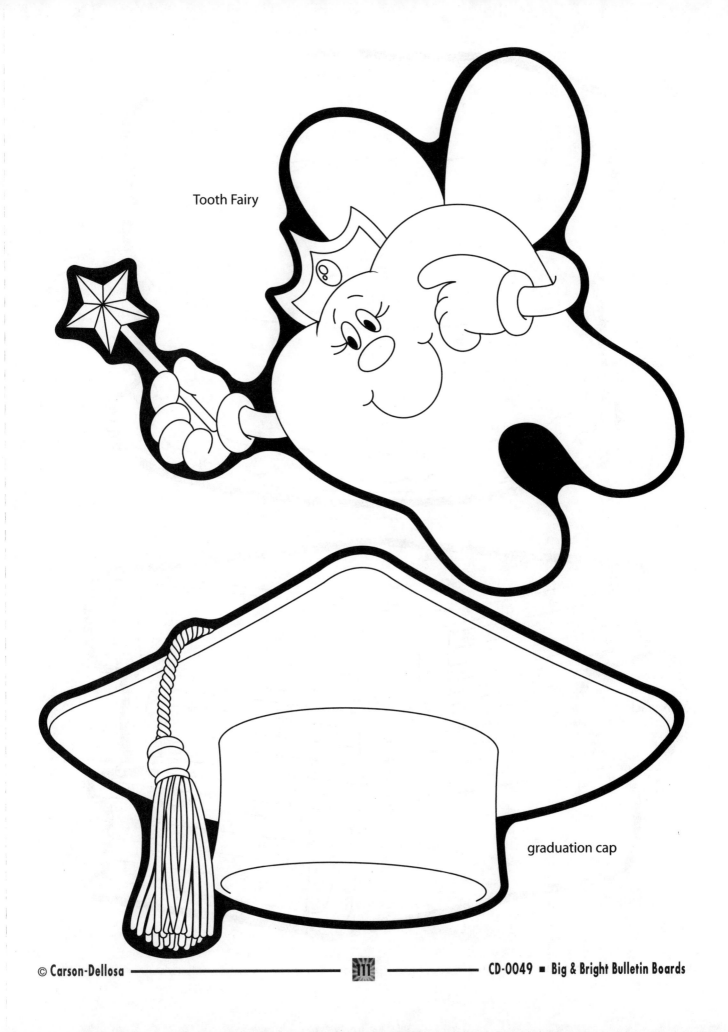

Tooth Fairy

graduation cap

cake

book stack

owl with books

baby mouse

CD-0049 ■ Big & Bright Bulletin Boards

seagull

lighthouse

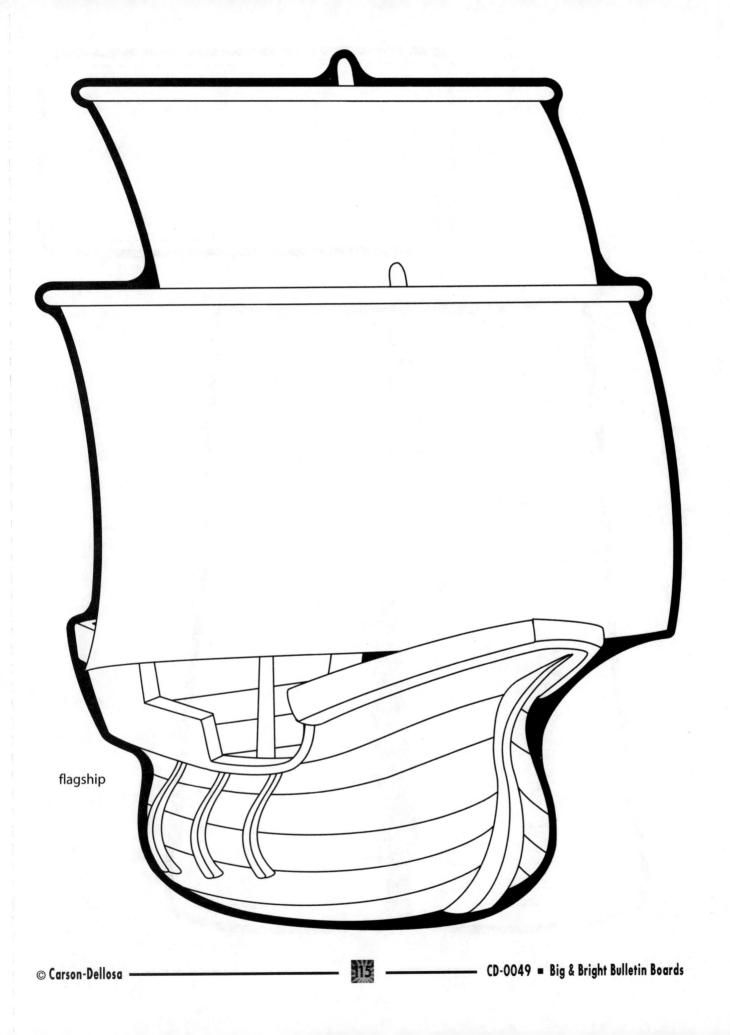

flagship

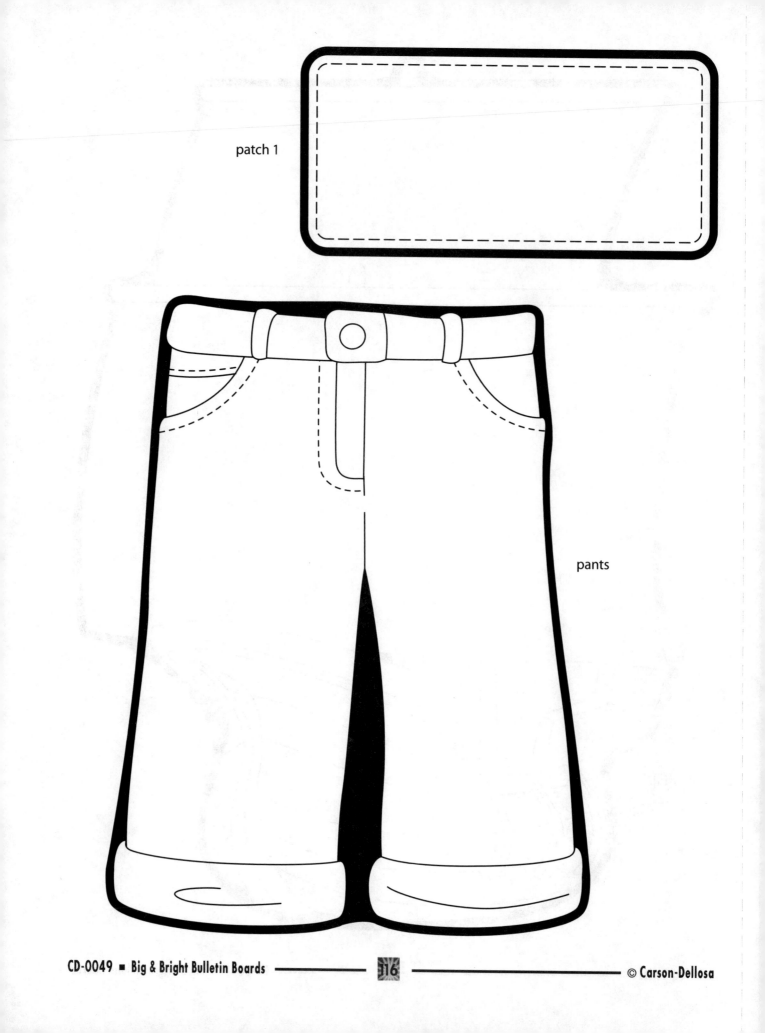

patch 1

pants

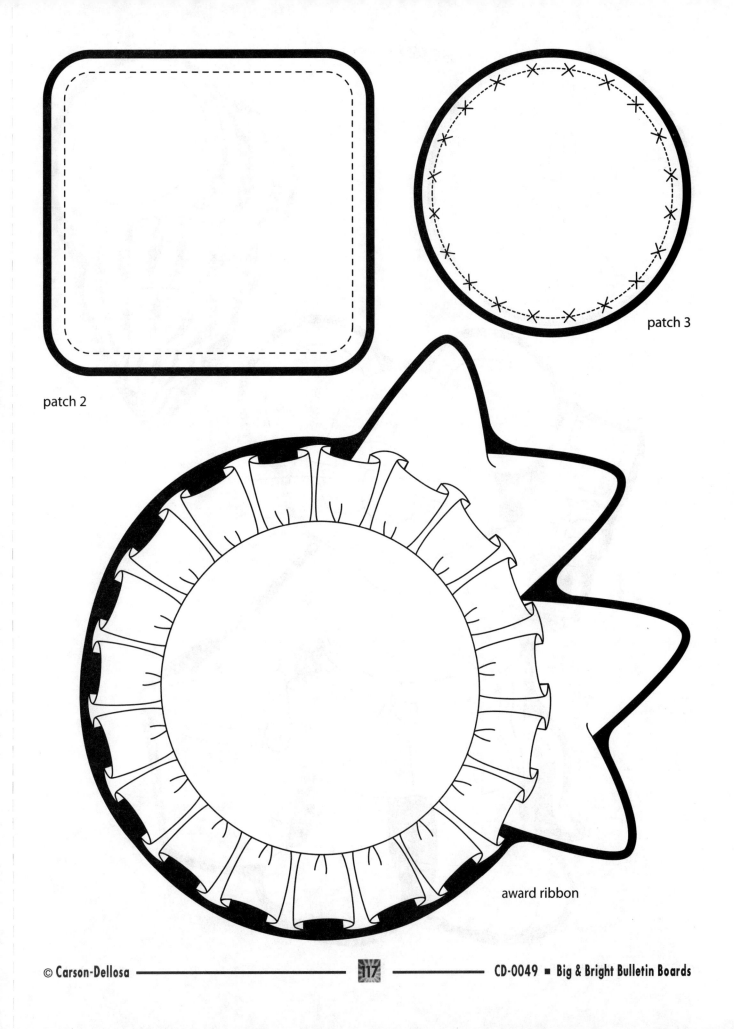

patch 2

patch 3

award ribbon

sand dollar

shell 1

beach mouse

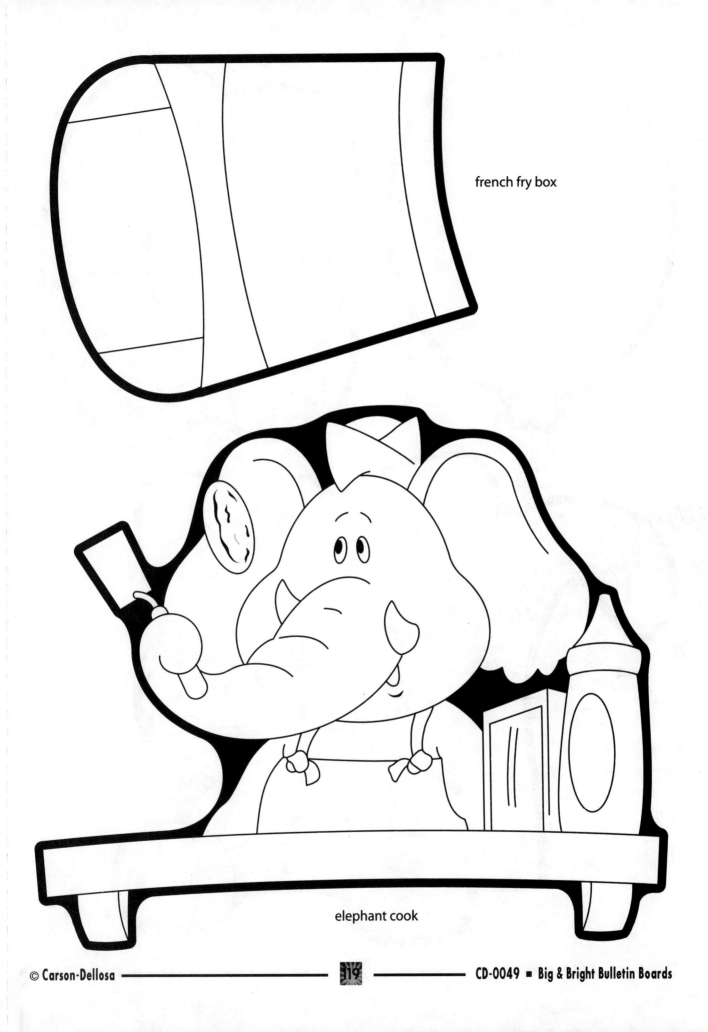

french fry box

elephant cook

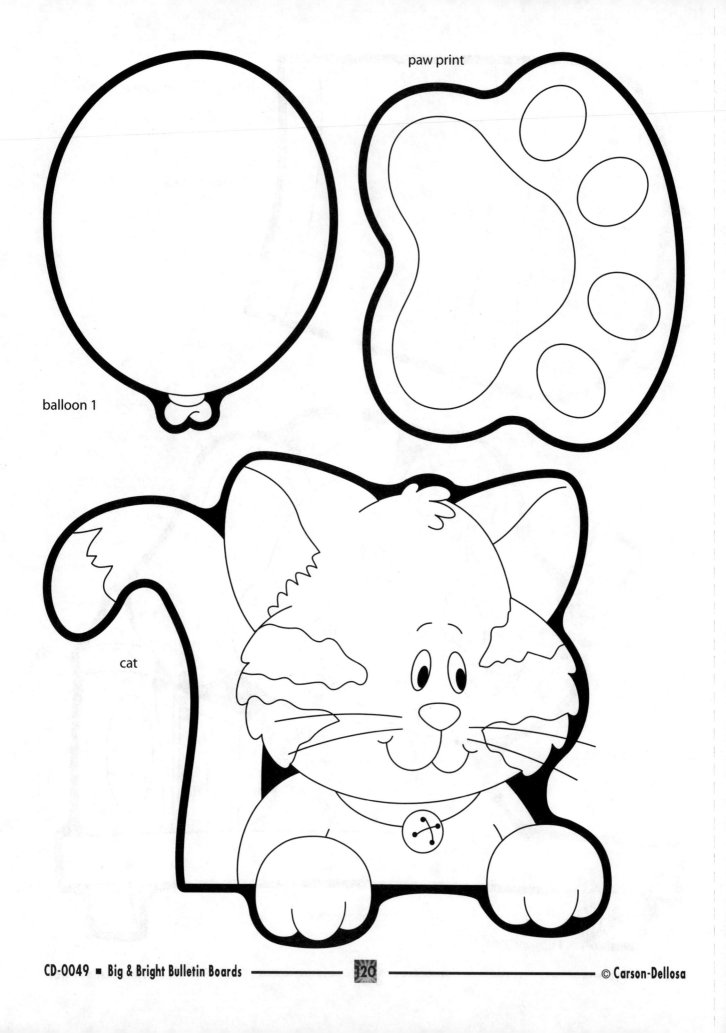

paw print

balloon 1

cat

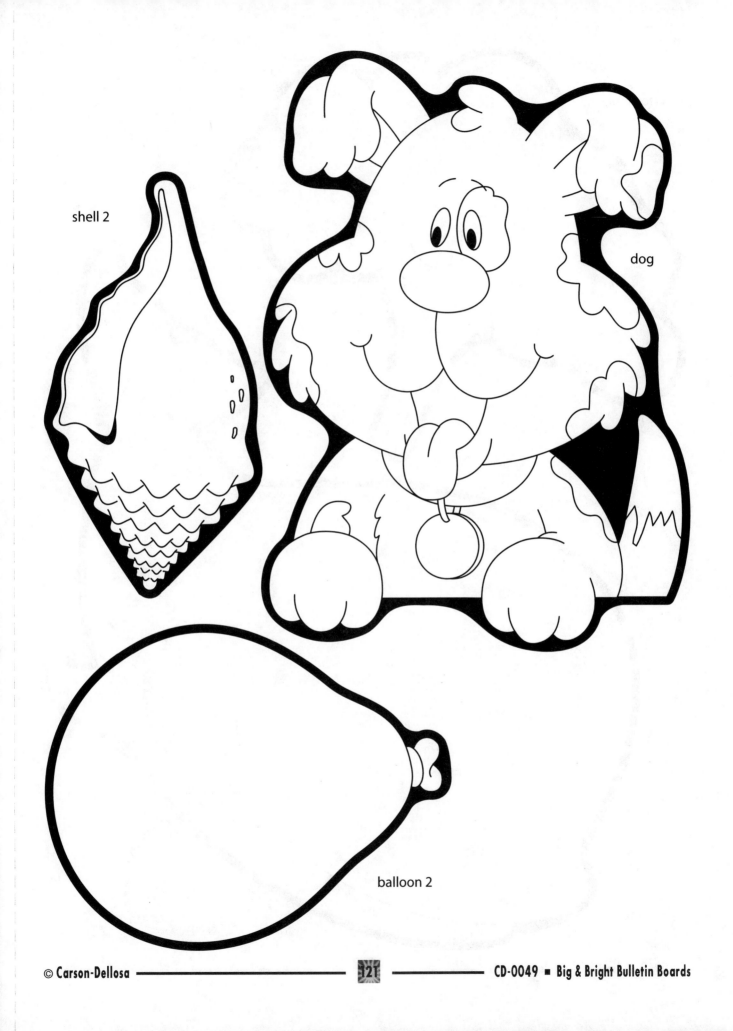

shell 2

dog

balloon 2

CD-0049 ■ Big & Bright Bulletin Boards

water spray

whale

clown

elephant and cat

watermelon

bus

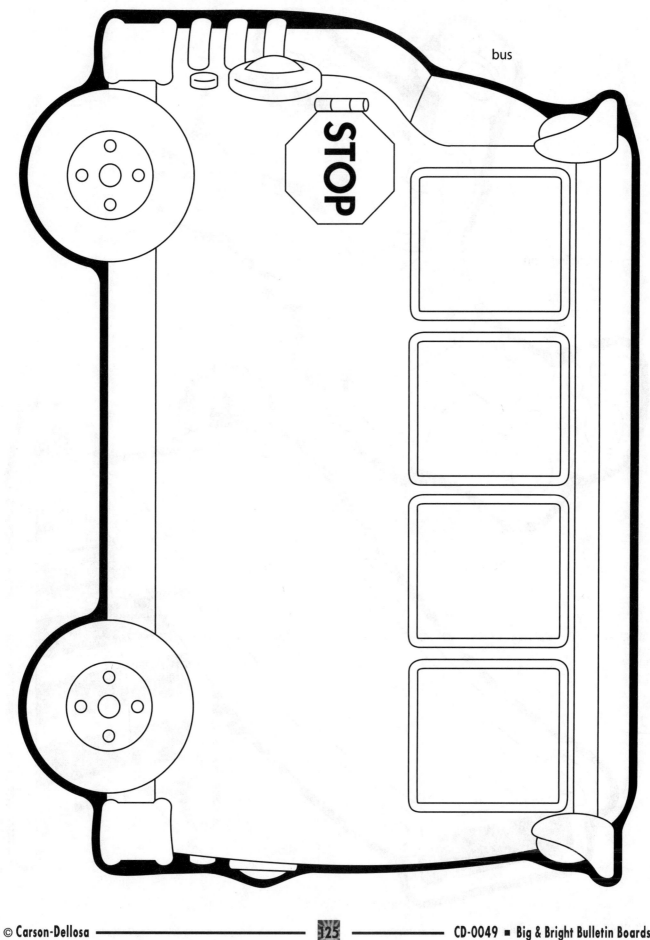

STOP

sliding dog

slide

worm

apple core

apple with bite

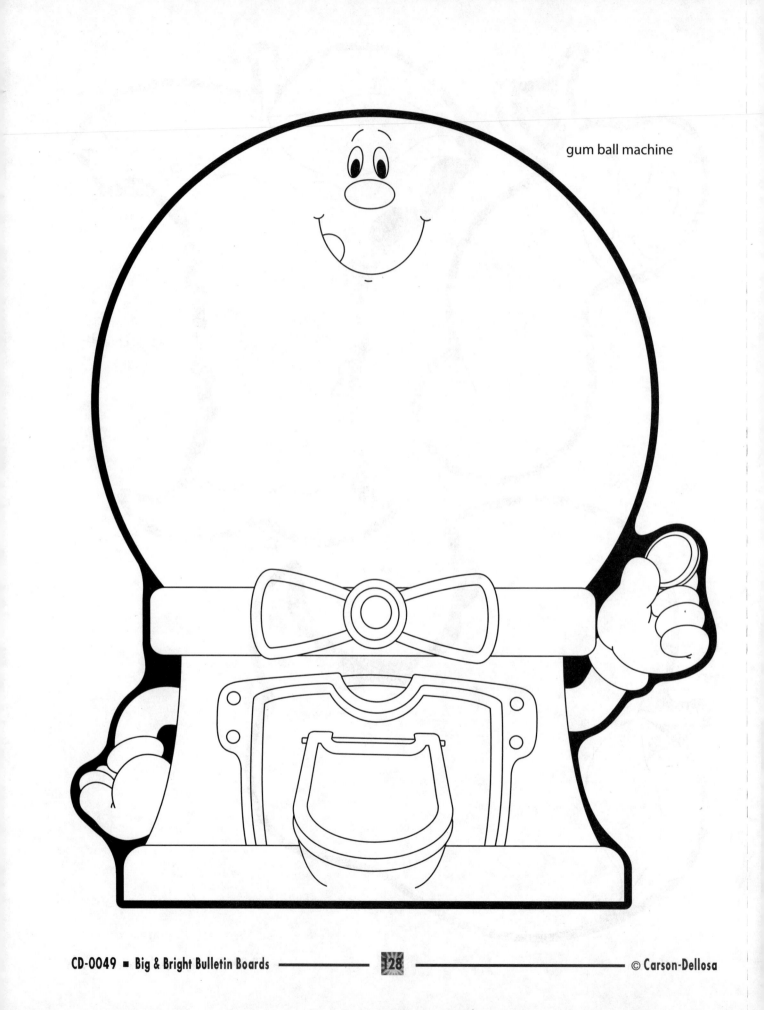

gum ball machine